PROPHECY IN PRACTICE

Pastor JIM PAUL is a member of the leadership team at the Airport Fellowship in Toronto. He travels widely to teach and preach, spreading the 'spiritual conflagration' and offering perspective and insight. 'There is no magic to the gift of prophecy. We all have to start at the feet of Jesus.'

CONTENTS

FOREWORD

Prophecy is one of the more visible gifts of the Holy Spirit that has come alive with the present renewal. Here at the Toronto Airport Christian Fellowship we have defined prophecy in terms of 1 Corinthians 14:3, 'But everyone that prophesies speaks to men for their strengthening, encouragement and comfort'. Put simply—prophecy is to build-up, lift-up and cheer-up!

This gift of the Spirit can also be very destructive if not pastored properly. Wild eyed prophets can roar through your church like Old Testament relics. They can release condemning and harsh words and leave behind a whirlwind. For this very reason, some in the Body of Christ have understandably turned away from this gift. Some would say, 'the downside is just too great'. It is true. However, let's not throw this baby out with the bath water. There is a great need for teaching on this subject. I'm glad that Jim Paul has brought out this timely book on *Prophecy in Practice*.

I have known Jim since 1987. He has always had that uncanny ability to receive words of knowledge for healing or prophetic encouragement. It has not always been smooth sailing. What ministry gift is? Pastoral correction and oversight is the only safe place for both the prophetically gifted person and the local church. For the past four years, Jim has been traveling the world, spreading 'The Father's Blessing'. Many of the amazing stories that you will read in this book come from his international ministry. The book is worth the price, just for the stories alone! The teaching value of this book is also excellent.

I have been blessed by the prophetic. This present move of the Holy Spirit in our church was described to us through reliable prophetic witnesses several months before the fateful day of January 20, 1994. I personally believe that God has the Church prophetically at the threshing floor. During this season He is breaking off that hard shell and preparing us to become 'food' for the nations. The word of the Lord is now in our hands so that we might feed hungry people. You will be fed, even challenged as you read Jim's book. His encounters with God may shake your comfort-zones and spur you on to be a stronger voice for the Master.

John Arnott, Senior Pastor
Toronto Airport Christian Fellowship
April 1998

INTRODUCTION

This book has been on my mind for a number of years. As a teenager I encountered God's voice while playing impromptu songs on the family piano. I had just rededicated my life to Christ and strange things began to happen to me. Invariably I would be the first one to get home from school and the house would be empty on many afternoons. It was just me and the piano, or so I thought. No one told me that my conversion experience would bring this added extra—God speaking to me. Later I learned that these were 'spiritual songs' according to Ephesians 5:19—songs which the Holy Spirit teaches us. Tears often flooded my eyes and would drop on the ivory keys as I would hear expressions of God's love for me in those little songs. They were actually prophetic songs, songs that carried the voice of God. I knew some day that I would have to write about those and other encounters with God's voice.

Writing a book on the prophetic gifts by no means qualifies me as infallible. In fact I am humbled when someone introduces me as a *prophet*. Mistakes and miscues have dogged my steps. Many of us have also been enrolled in OJT College—that is the college of 'On the Job Training'. Our commission to make disciples assumes this process of learning. We get to learn as we go on in this Christian life. John Arnott, senior pastor at Toronto Airport Christian Fellowship, has kept me on a short leash. If you are not in one of those wonderful pastoral-prophetic relationships, seek the Lord to provide one for you.

I trust that through this book you will sense both the power and tenderness of God's voice—a very interesting combination! I once thought that power was mutually exclusive of tenderness. Not so with our heavenly Father. His voice is strong enough to shake heaven and earth, and yet Scripture tells us that 'he will quiet you with his love, he will rejoice over you with singing' (Zephaniah 3:17). Both power and tenderness find their greatest expression in the Father's voice. A new day has dawned on the Church and the Father of 'the bride' is speaking afresh.

I have sought to illuminate the various ways his voice can come to you and through you. Some of the ways may possibly be new. Don't discount them because you have never encountered them. Both through the means of biblical exposition and personal illustration, a full range of prophetic gifts will be discussed. In the tenth chapter, 'The Prophetic in Revival History', we will see that the new really is old. Revelations, the foretelling of events and ecstatic prophecies, to mention only a few, are a part of the Church's history. Somehow we have been distanced from our heritage. It's time to have 'prophecy in practice'.

1

GOD'S PROPHETIC ARMY

It was my son's birthday and his party was to be at a local Toronto shopping mall where there was an indoor fair with all the rides and candy floss a boy could want. I got the job of driving him and his friends to this parent trap, and after having dropped him off there, I bided my time while he and his friends played. What relief I felt when I found a McDonald's overlooking the indoor park. My next three hours were meticulously planned: extra large coffee in hand, Bible and note pad at my side and the whole afternoon to prepare for church. Little did I know that a church was about to take place in this hamburger heaven.

Hamburger heaven

Just when I thought I was settled for the time being, a man and woman sat down on the table next to me. The man was clutching his stomach as his wife tended to his constant groans. I knew it wasn't a bad hamburger he had eaten, since they had only just walked into the restaurant.

I couldn't help but hear Ralph's* agony and their discussion to call a taxi for a quick journey home or to the hospital. Eavesdropping is quite an easy thing to do at such close quarters.

Then, in that still small place of my heart, the Lord spoke to me. For me, this speaking of the Lord takes place in the arena of my heart and not my ears. I have never heard an audible voice that I could say was God speaking to me. However, I do know that he does speak to me and many others, maybe even you, in the form of an inner conviction. At times it's as real as an audible voice. It can be so clear that you enter into a dialogue with the Spirit of God. The one speaking is the Holy Spirit who indwells every believer and who mediates all of God's benefits to us. So when I use this term, 'the Lord spoke', I mean an inner impression or thought that comes with authority.

The Lord asked me a simple question: 'Well, are you going to pray for him?' I blurted out a quiet response: 'Who me, here, right now? I'm getting ready for church!' While the Lord and I were in the midst of one of those no-win creator-creature discussions, Ralph moved to the other side of the restaurant and stretched out on the bench. 'Oh no,' I thought with horror, 'he's going to die!' My coffee, Bible and notebook were abandoned on the table where I had been hiding and I rushed to the other side of McDonald's. Looking straight at him I asked, 'Would you let me pray for you?' 'Yes, that would be all right,' came the answer.

Have you ever noticed that unbelievers can be more willing to let you pray for them than we are courageous enough to ask them? By this time Ralph had pulled himself up to a seated position. Perhaps he thought that it was disrespectful to have someone pray for you while in a

*pseudonym

horizontal position. I asked him to open his hands to receive a touch from the Lord and I simply prayed, 'Come, Holy Spirit.' Did he ever come! Ralph slid back again to the bench under the weight of his presence. I continued to pray for healing over his abdomen with a clear conviction that Jesus loves to show himself strong to wounded lambs that need a shepherd. An overview of the Gospels shows that Jesus generally didn't pray for healing for the righteous. It was the prostitutes (Matthew 21:31), tax collectors (Matthew 11:19) and foreigners (John 4:4–42) that he often sought out. Ralph was being pursued by the Saviour.

While he was lying there on the restaurant bench, I knew that God had not finished. At that point I was stirred to prophesy over this precious man. I sensed in my spirit that God wanted to give him a message; maybe even a message to unravel the root of his sickness. 'You've been running from God all your life,' I said to him. 'He's been calling you and calling you to serve him and you have refused to listen. But he's speaking to you again.' Then without warning his wife began to dance, lift her hands and shout out loud in that busy restaurant. 'Oweee, Ralph, did you hear that? He's speaking the very words your mother just spoke to you when you left her at the airport a few minutes ago.'

I looked sheepishly around the restaurant to see if the noise and the dancing had disturbed any of the patrons. You don't usually get such a response after eating a hamburger at McDonald's, no matter what the TV commercials may say. No one seemed to notice the proceedings.

'What church do you come from?' she asked, as her husband was standing beside her. I responded the best I could, giving her the name of the Toronto Airport Christian Fellowship and some basic directions. Then, after thanking me for my care, the couple walked out into the shopping mall. They came into the restaurant very troubled. They left smiling. The gut-wrenching pain had gone. Instead of calling for an ambulance, they went shopping! One simple desire to bless a sick man and speak words of counsel to him had visible results. Little did I know that I would be repeating the same sermon that a godly mother had just preached to her wandering son. I had a real church service that afternoon in hamburger heaven. This experience is not just for me—it's for everyone. Such a freedom is coming to speak God's heart to the lost in the body of Christ that restaurants around the world will become 'church' for many who have never seen a stained-glass window or hymn book. The Holy Spirit's anointing is making us a bold, prophetic people.

Party at Tim Horton's

The Holy Spirit also likes to visit doughnut shops. Tim Horton's is the Rolls Royce of all the doughnut shops in Canada, in my opinion. Believe me, we have a legion of different franchise operations, but Tim Horton's seems to be at every major intersection in the country. A group of about twenty, from the Scarborough Vineyard Christian Fellowship, visited one of these Tim Horton's on a Friday night in April 1994.

After four months of continual renewal meetings at the Toronto Airport Christian Fellowship, the 'blessing' was now spreading to other churches in the region. Scarborough is a borough of the city of Toronto and a church had been planted there recently by the Airport Fellowship. Paul White, senior pastor of Scarborough Vineyard, asked me to come and conduct some renewal meetings in his area of the city.

Being a relatively new church, they did not have a building solely at their disposal. That night a school gymnasium was used for the special service and all went well until the janitor began to pace the floor. A bad sign. We had just begun to minister to the folk when we ran out of allotted time and had to end our renewal meeting. One by one we loaded the believers, who were in various states of rapture, into each of the vehicles. Paul approached me and asked if I wanted to go out to Tim Horton's for a coffee and doughnut, realising that the night was still young. What red-blooded Canadian could refuse such an offer? Canadians per capita eat more doughnuts than any other nation in the world.

I was the second car to arrive from the service at the local franchise (the congregation had overheard us talking, and the word spread). As I entered, Lori, one of the church members who had been at the service, waved me over to her table.

'Jim, come over here . . . You won't believe what just happened. I went to order my coffee and doughnut and I just fell on the floor and began to shake. I had to crawl up the cabinet that held the fancy doughnuts in front of the cashier in order to explain to the clerk that Jesus was touching me. I then walked back to my seat, vibrating with food in hand.'

As far as I could see, the vibrating had not subsided because all three ladies were now bouncing in their seats.

The apostle John describes his own powerful encounter with Jesus in Revelation 1:17—'When I saw him, I fell at his feet as though dead.' Daniel, the Old Testament prophet, has a similar testimony: 'Then I heard him speaking, and as I listened to him, I fell into a deep sleep, my face to the ground. A hand touched me and set me trembling on my hands and knees' (Daniel 10:9–10). We are coming to understand some of the scriptures that describe phenomena that can take place when one meets with God. Lori just happened to encounter God's presence in the public eye.

After everyone had arrived at the scene, ministry time began in earnest. Some were laughing, others shaking, and some others were sliding to the floor as they blessed each other unashamedly. You see, many of us had just made a covenant with God at the Sunday night mega rally with Randy Clark, the pastor of the St Louis Vineyard. He had been instrumental in bringing the fire of renewal to our church during the early days of 1994. At that rally, we committed ourselves to the Lord that we would let the Holy Spirit come upon us at any time, at any place, in any way. He heard every prayer that was uttered those five days before, and now we were experiencing a major outpouring of his sweet presence in the midst of a doughnut shop.

There were at least ten unbelievers in the restaurant that night watching the event. The reactions were varied. Some watched indifferently, others didn't even notice the added noise. (Doughnut shops seem to have a tolerance for people noise.) One man in a black leather jacket was quietly seated at a table with three lady friends, peering at us through the plastic plants that separated the various booths. I was able to hold back the constant waves of God's presence that were flowing over me until Paul Goudy, the associate pastor, was shaken much like the action of a jack hammer all around the hall and finally came to land in front of the cashier. From that vantage point he began to prophesy in a loud voice and with great trembling: 'I'm a carpenter. I don't usually do this but the

Lord wants to speak to you to about his love and plan for your life . . .'

It was useless to resist God's power any longer and I fell back in my seat, feet dangling in mid air over the edge of the bench. One girl from the church began witnessing about Jesus and gave a running commentary about the various manifestations to those seated at the adjoining tables. Young and old alike were willing to listen. Then the police showed up!

By that time I was in a half-erect position, but my face was glued to the table. I was literally unable to move from that awkward position. I thought for sure that the paddy wagon had arrived and we were all on our way to the police station. I could hear Paul Goudy explaining to the policeman, while pointing his finger in good fun, 'It was Jim Paul's fault, he was the preacher tonight!' To my great surprise, the policeman walked right past us into the toilet where he arrested a teenager probably involved in a drug deal. Then he walked out, passing us again in full view of the proceedings.

God had blinded his eyes! Or perhaps the policeman had other things to worry about with a young offender being dragged along at his side. But for us, party time began in earnest. We couldn't help but celebrate our deliverance. Some of the church ladies began to dance the jig in the aisle, while others just laughed with God's joy. One of the ladies at the table with the man in the black leather jacket began laughing with us. She told us that at about the age of five she had given her life to the Lord at Sunday school, yet had been away from him for many years. But that night, in the midst of the holy laughter, she felt the Lord calling her back to himself. 'O Lord, give Jim a prophecy for this place.' I responded by saying something to the effect that I was incapable of receiving such a blessing.

The honest fact was that I had just witnessed how strongly the Holy Spirit had shaken a prophecy out of the other pastor, and frankly I was not ready for such answered prayer. He continued praying and suddenly I heard the Lord speak to me. 'The man dressed in black leathers has injured his back in an accident and Jim, I want you to pray for his healing.' When I agreed to speak this word of knowledge, I was immediately freed from my frozen position on the table and I was able to approach this man. Touching his back lightly, I repeated what the Lord had said and then witnessed what seemed to be like a bolt of electricity going through his body. It looked like God had just healed him.

By now it was 12.20 am and I left that hallowed place to go home to my family. The other folks from the church stayed up until 2.00 am, explaining the Scriptures and the manifest power of God. A few weeks later my black-jacketed acquaintance came forward during one Sunday morning service in the Scarborough Vineyard and publicly confessed the Lord Jesus as his Saviour. This Jesus was the one who so radically confronted him at his local doughnut restaurant through a 'prophetic church'.

If there was ever a day that the Church was needed to rise up as God's mouthpiece it is today. Erma Bombeck, the editor of the North-American-based news magazine *USA Today*, clearly describes the world dilemma in the 12 August 1992 issue: 'People are going crazy because there's no stability here any more in their lives. There's no anchor. No centre. People don't seem to have something they can hang on to and believe in any more. People are really confused and they've lost their way.'[1]

Jesus is the 'anchor for the soul' (Hebrews 6:19). We do have a great hope, a great salvation and a great message. But something has gone wrong with the 'harvest'. Lost souls are not finding their way to Jesus in record numbers in the Western world, despite their desperate condition. We're in a spiritual battle! Gains on this field of combat have been meagre for several reasons, I believe. One reason is that the Church at large has been unwilling to pray. Lost and broken people need to be drawn to the Saviour by all-out intercession. The church in Argentina has shown us how united, fervent prayer has literally brought revival to that nation where hundreds are being saved every day.[2] A classic example of the power of prayer as it relates to reaching people is the Yoido Full Gospel Church of Seoul, Korea. After a recent visit to this church, I quickly discerned why this assembly is growing by thousands per month and now numbers well over 700,000 members. Dr David Yonggi Cho began the church in 1958 with only a $50 tent and a call to pray. He personally prays three hours a day and all of the church members pray a minimum of one hour a day and much more when they pray through the night at one of many concerts of prayer during the week.[3] Jesus did say 'Ask the Lord of the harvest, therefore, to send out workers into his harvest field'. (Matthew 9:38).

In this verse I believe we see another key for this battle. The failure is not only our lack of prayer, but also our lack of proclamation. The workers must do their part. God's Spirit is now delivering us from that persistent curse of 'lock jaw' disease. You know the sickness of which I speak—the one that silences the mouth when we leave the confines of the church and enter into the world. However, the renewing power of the Holy Spirit is bringing a new boldness on the Church, and it's about time.

In a recent edition of *Perspectives* magazine, there is a concise call to arms for every Spirit-filled Christian. The article analyses the prophetic gift as follows:

The Old Testament prophet has given place to the New Testament Christian who may experience various degrees of prophetic activity. Instead of a few selected men and women giving earth-shaking prophecies of eternal proportions, we have the entire people of God—the Church—as a community of prophetic people who are mutually filled with the Holy Spirit.[4]

The Holy Spirit is filling up God's prophetic people for what I believe is the last battle—the battle for the hearts of 2.5 billion people who have not as yet turned to the Lord. We have a story to tell the nations with attesting signs that follow the Gospel proclamation (Mark 16:17), signs of healing, revelation, love and power.

'The gifts of the Spirit,' Winkie Pratney maintains, 'are the wrath of God on the works of Satan.'[5] They are his declaration of war against isolation, disease and sin. They are not charismatic toys! We need the gift of prophecy in the Church, but we need this precious manifestation of God's Spirit even more in the world. Not everyone can give or receive a prophetic word each Sunday. Time just doesn't allow for it. But there is a broken world outside our door with time on its hands. The Holy Spirit is anointing us for it. Whether his anointing comes upon you in your corner shop or in a local fast-food restaurant, it doesn't matter—the Spirit likes them all. That's because the lost go there, plenty of them.

This book is, in essence, a review of the prophetic release that has been witnessed during these years of renewal. It's not just a retelling of the story of our church, the Toronto Airport Christian Fellowship, the well-head of the so-called 'Toronto blessing'. It's the story of the body of Christ. An anointing to hear God and in turn speak out his heart has been seen in practically every church where the outpouring is welcomed. Almost from the beginning of this visitation of God's presence in our Toronto church, I've had the privilege of preaching in many nations. From across Canada and the United States, from Mexico and the United Kingdom, from Korea to Taiwan, from Germany to Iceland, similar prophetic manifestations have appeared. Throughout our journey together, these stories from around the world will be considered in the light of the biblical and historical record. God is not silent! From cover to cover, the Bible describes our God as one who speaks by his Spirit. He is a self-revealing God. He also speaks to us through church history where prophetic words, visions and signs were common during days of revival. God is revisiting us and we need to be ready.

I trust that this book will be a marker along the road as you walk with the almighty. You may have had prophetic encounters with God that remained in the realm of the unspoken or unexplained. Maybe you have discounted some of these encounters with your speaking God. Our Christian society looks somewhat askance at those who have had mountain-top experiences. 'You are so heavenly minded that you're no earthly good' is a common rebuttal to one's prophetic interactions with God. It's with that in mind that I hope these personal stories of believers from around the world will find a home in your heart, if not your experience.

Our God is a speaking God and let me encourage you that he does want to speak to you and through you. Be encouraged by the mandate of 1 Corinthians 14:31—'for you can *all* prophesy' (my italics). We will discuss this verse along with other supporting scriptures that testify that you can be a voice for God. In the final analysis, I trust that you will believe God for revelatory words in your own world where you live. Let God's prophetic Church arise!

2

A VISITATION OF THE SPIRIT

Henderson Hospital, which is perched on top of the escarpment in Hamilton, Ontario, is a special place for me. Not only was it my birthplace some forty-five years ago, but it was also the site from where I began to encounter God, albeit vicariously.

I was my father's first son and he knew what the Scriptures taught regarding first sons—they were given to the Lord (Exodus 34:19). He was also a first son and his mother, my grandmother, Mary Paul made sure that my father knew that he was given to the Lord for his work. This never transpired, but the wish remained in my dad's heart. As a result, when I was born, my earthly father physically lifted me up before the heavenly father in a prophetic act, and gave me away.

I was a marked man. My teenage rebellion ended abruptly when I was fifteen, thanks to the prayers and persistence of a godly mother. She persuaded me to go to church that eventful Sunday when I both heard and felt God calling me to the Saviour. My heart was pounding like a drum inside my chest as the evangelist waited for sinners to come forward. The battle raged in my bones because I refused to be embarrassed in front of the church. Finally, I got home and there on the floor of my bedroom I cried out to Jesus to save me. New life flooded me from that day on.

Being converted and baptised in a conservative evangelical church had its own set of joys and challenges. At times I heard sermons against the 'Pentecostals'. The pastor would say to the youth, 'I don't want you going to those "Holy Roller" churches.' I couldn't imagine it: rolling on the floor of the church? But now I know! I even toed the party line as the president of the youth group and would spout the doctrine of the church.

The path was set. I was on my way to Bible school and might possibly enter the conservative evangelical ministry. Then came the stern realisation that there was a 'Pentecostal' in my house! My mother had changed. She said that she had been baptised in the Spirit and now spoke in tongues. This budding young dispensationalist was radically challenged when I went to one of her Friday night charismatic house-church meetings. They had a passion for God and for life. The gifts of the Spirit, which I thought had died out with the last apostle, were flowing that night. Indeed, prophetic messages were given at each meeting and I knew in my heart that it was from God and that he was encouraging his people. The summer of my first year at Bible school, I too became one of those charismatics, but I was not prepared for what was about to happen in our church some twenty-two years later.

All of life is touched when God comes close to you. He has come very close to us at the Toronto Airport Christian Fellowship since 20 January 1994, and more than a million people from around the world have joined at least one of our nightly celebrations. The one thing that clearly stands out in my mind is the strength of God's voice. For me, this is the undeniable evidence that God has intersected our lives.

The intimate whisper of God's Spirit challenges all the other voices that have kept us away from people, ourselves and ultimately him. Time and again visitors get up from our church carpet and testify to an intimate dialogue with the living God. We have received literally thousands of thank-you letters and testimonials that describe the life changes that took place when God spoke to people during their stay with us. As a result, some have cried, some have laughed and some have trembled or even prophesied in Jesus' name.

When you think about it, this whole present movement does in some way revolve around prophecy. But this is not the same as those 'end of the world' predictions which claim to foretell calamities or fortunes. 'But everyone who prophesies,' Paul defines, 'speaks to men for their strengthening, encouragement and comfort' (1 Corinthians 14:3). That kind of uplifting prophecy breaks into our darkness, causing us to live again. This is God's intimate voice to us. He speaks to the core of our being about his unconditional love and we are comforted. Many have responded to this matchless encounter with the Holy Spirit and have become prophetic people both in church and in the world where they live and work.

Prophecy by definition is the voice of God mediated through his people by a gift of the Holy Spirit (1 Corinthians 12:9–10), bringing both edification and correction (1 Corinthians 14:3), direction and commissioning (1 Timothy 1:18). At the outset, I am suggesting that God is at the bottom of this outpouring of revelation. It was his plan throughout the ages to have his people speak on his behalf. By no means does this negate the voice of

God in the Scriptures. When God speaks through his people it will only confirm the teaching of the word. Anything else is to be discarded.

Now don't get me wrong! Just because someone has been overcome by the Spirit in one of the meetings and prophesies, doesn't mean they now walk around with a capital 'P' prophet label. There is a training time required by God for such a lofty calling. John Sandford suggests in his ground-breaking book on the prophetic gift, *The Elijah Task*, that 'it shall probably take no less than a dozen years' to be released into the office of a prophet.[6] With that bit of news please don't throw this book out the window! There are three increasing levels of prophetic practice according to Graham Cooke in his book *Developing Your Prophetic Gifting*. They are the gift of prophecy, prophetic ministry and the prophetic office.[7] We need to commit to the process. We have the opportunity to grow in the prophetic gifting.

God is releasing en masse the gift of prophecy in the body of Christ. He is mobilising an army, a prophetic church, that will declare by life and words the intent of God's heart. He's restoring truth and hope in the nations through a bold prophetic people.

My own story

This is my own story, as I have viewed the outpouring at the Toronto Airport Christian Fellowship from the beginning, and as I have travelled as a pastor from the church to several continents. I have witnessed similar revelatory or prophetic messages being released as the presence of Jesus came into the meeting place. Revelation 19:10 (KJV) says that 'the testimony of Jesus is the spirit of prophecy'. Simply put, 'where Jesus is being lifted up there comes a freedom on the congregation to both hear and speak God's heart'.

Everyone has their own story of how, when and where God's blessing came to them. Some can point to a specific place on the carpet in our church where they fell into the 'everlasting arms'. Others can even pinpoint the exact time when the Holy Spirit overwhelmed them. My story goes like this.

On 20 January 1994, I ran out of the back door of our church building, scared silly. I didn't want anyone to see my discontent, not to mention the fact that I was frightened by the display of power. I knew the anointing was of God, but I didn't want the package it came in. Did believers have to fall on the floor? Did they have to laugh hilariously? Did they have to shake violently? I had been a charismatic since I was nineteen and I'd never seen the likes of this. With no personal history of falling on the floor in the Spirit, I couldn't appreciate the experience. I almost fell once when a zealous preacher laid a heavy finger on my forehead and I lost my balance. I was sure that his thumb print was indelibly stamped on the centre of my forehead. It had left a bad taste in my mouth and spirit. To say the least, I ran!

However, the 'hound of heaven', God's Spirit, arrested me in my car as I attempted to drive home. 'Three times Jim . . . I want you to receive prayer three times tomorrow night from Randy Clark!' The Spirit's voice thundered in my heart. He meant business and I knew better than to argue.

It was Friday night, 21 January, a night to remember. Randy Clark preached an impassioned message on the 'prodigal son' and called us to come home to the Father. I jumped to my feet and round one shortly commenced as Randy prayed for me. It seemed like hours. 'Surely the whole church must be watching me standing here like a bump on a log,' I muttered to myself. My hands had been open, waiting for lightning to hit me and nothing was happening. Finally, I felt the Spirit's presence and heard God's soft voice of love. He spoke to a broken little boy inside and brought me back to life. I had been obese for a long period of my childhood. Names like 'fatty', 'jumbo' and 'pig' were burnt into my mental computer, spoiling any hope for peace. But the Father now spoke his love much louder than the taunts of the children. I got out of the bunk house that night—that's the place where prodigal sons and daughters relegate themselves when they return to the Father's house thinking themselves absolutely unworthy of forgiveness. Also, the wall that was supporting me didn't do its job. I had been receiving prayer in the aisle beside the wall and I eventually slid down the wall and ended up on the floor.

Round two began through simple obedience. I was lying on the floor in perfect peace, staring up at the bottom of a chair labelled 'Made in Canada'. I could have lain there in God's presence for the rest of my adult life. This was sweet and healing, yet the night had just begun. I was on a mission. On my feet again, I found a place at the front. Randy came over and prayed for me once more. This time no waiting for thunder. Without notice, I started 'pogo-ing' non-stop for ages in the centre aisle, then 'hit the deck'.

Have you noticed the new vocabulary in the Church? Words like 'pogo-ing', 'hit the deck', 'carpet time', 'drunk', etc are used to describe the manifestations. I like the expression heard in Scotland, 'Jehovah Zappa'. A rough interpretation is 'God of the electric shock'! That's what happened to me—I was electrocuted by liquid love.

Round three was soon to come. I scraped myself off the floor, absolutely overcome by the power of God's love. Wobbling like a dazed prize fighter refusing to give up, I asked for the third instalment. Randy graciously heard my plea and gave wise counsel as I crashed through two rows of chairs. This time I stayed down.

Our training and deployment of catchers was woefully lacking in those early days. No bumps or bruises showed, but there was a deep sense of joy that cascaded over my heart and out of my lips. I was overflowing with the Spirit's power when a video camera glared in my face; that was for posterity. We didn't know when the Spirit's outpouring would stop, so every encounter was recorded as proof that God had intersected with our little church at the end of the runway. I'm forever grateful that he arrested me before I ran away from this personal, life-changing interaction with the most high. His voice is like thunder!

Over the years he has thundered time and time again in the hearts of his children. He has done that before. John recounts the Bethsaida experience when the Father spoke from heaven over his Son Jesus, days before the cross. 'The crowd that was there and heard it said it had thundered' (John 12:29). When God brings some revelation it is much like thunder. God wakes us from our sleep and we come to life.

In the following chapters we will review the common thread of revelatory gifting that appears when the Holy Spirit is welcomed. 'Come Holy Spirit' is not a glib invocation you may employ to bless a Sunday service. He is the very life blood of the Church. He wants the Father's voice to be heard through the gift of prophecy, visions, dreams, angelic visitations, prophetic signs and prophetic song and art.

This is not some lunatic fringe experience. These signs and manifestations have their foundation in the biblical record and have been witnessed in historical revival movements. A new day has dawned for the bride of Christ and she is being made ready to bring in the 'harvest'. But first we must learn to listen to the whisper of God's Spirit. Let's crawl up into the Father's arms and let him teach us the art of listening, because hearing his voice is the foundation of prophecy itself.

Hearing God

Surely God is the greatest 'prophet' and hearing God is the basis for all the prophetic gifts in his people. In light of the Old and New Testaments, another definition of prophecy is 'that which reveals God's heart and purposes as it relates to life, both personal and corporate'. Throughout Scripture one can see the 'blessed Trinity'—Father, Son and Spirit—revealing the divine purpose. The Father has been speaking to mankind since the garden of Eden. Even when Adam's first son was on the brink of rebellion, God came near with his presence and his voice and warned Cain that 'sin is crouching at your door' (Genesis 4:7).

Furthermore, the task of the Saviour was to reveal, explain and declare God to us. That is the essence of John 1:18—'No-one has ever seen God, but God the One and Only, who is at the Father's side, has made him known.' He is the fulfilment of Moses' promise in Deuteronomy 18:15—'God will raise up for you a prophet.' He did not speak or work on his own, but only spoke as the Father taught him and did what he saw the Father doing (John 8:28; 5:19).[8]

The Holy Spirit also operates under the 'prophetic mantle' that is resident in the Godhead. In the upper room discourse, Jesus described the revelatory mandate of the comforter in that 'he will not speak on his own; he will speak only what he hears, and he will tell you what is yet to come' (John 16:13). If Jesus and the Holy Spirit needed to listen to the Father's voice before anything could be done or said, how much more so we, who are called to 'go into all the world'?

We too have the great privilege of hearing God. Martin Luther staked his life on it! Rather than an elite group of priests hearing God on our behalf, we know the 'priesthood of all believers'. 'He has made us to be a kingdom of priests' (Revelation 1:6, KJV). We hear Jesus' voice as he calls us (John 6:44). We also hear the Spirit's voice and in turn call back to God as 'Abba' or 'Daddy' as children would say (Romans 8:15). We each have our own way of hearing God. For you maybe it's like Elijah's cave experience of the 'still small voice' (1 Kings 19:12). For others God will talk to them personally through a voice of scripture. For still others, God has provided a technicolor, full-blown vision.

Hearing with your eyes?

Yes, you can also hear with your eyes! While in a small group meeting one night, God said to me, 'Jim, look at the coffee table.' A strange directive when you're seated in a circle in someone's living room. You are not there as a furniture appraiser but as a worshipper. However, I obeyed the Spirit's nudge, and I watched as the wood grain became a living picture of raging waves with a child at the point of death in the midst. During a quiet moment following the worship I asked, 'Is there anyone here who almost drowned as a child?' There was dead silence for a moment and then a lady responded to the word. She retold a sad story from her childhood when she almost drowned in the North Sea. After living with that trauma for many years, God came to her that night through a word of knowledge and ministered to her broken heart.

It was also revealed that her body was afflicted with arthritis. A young girl in the house meeting went over and simply laid her hands over those arthritic hands and prayed for healing. The word/vision about the waves was just a door of opportunity for the Holy Spirit to bring a tangible blessing. 'Oh, the pain is gone,' she exclaimed, as that lady, a first-time visitor, was loved by God's people. Hearing with the eyes was the way in.

Saints in the Scriptures also heard with their eyes. Take for instance Amos's experience (Amos 8:1–6). One day the Lord dropped a vision of a basket of ripe fruit before him, then engaged him in dialogue. This is important to note because visions or pictures at the best of times need explanation. 'What do you see, Amos?' the Lord asked. 'A basket of fruit,' he answered. Then the Lord began to apply this earthly vision in a spiritual sense to the nation of Israel.

Learning to listen

Believers constantly come to me asking for a prophetic word thinking that I have one of the few telephone lines to heaven. I often respond by smiling, holding up my Bible and saying, 'Here is your word!' 2 Timothy 3:16 does say that 'all Scripture is God-breathed and is useful for teaching, rebuking, correcting and training in righteousness'. Learn to listen to God's word.

Recently, someone asked me for an interpretation of a vision. I felt it right to respond, 'He'll speak to you.' Sure enough, within a few minutes that person came back and blurted out, 'He did, he did, God explained the vision to me!' Get soaked in God's Spirit. He will speak volumes to you because he is preparing a massive army that will hear the commander's voice and do his bidding.

Let me give you some practical suggestions in this whole matter of hearing God's voice. First, don't be in a hurry. Take a lesson from the prophet Habakkuk. He said, 'I will stand at my watch and station myself on the ramparts; I will look to see what he will say to me, and what answer I am to give to this complaint' (Habakkuk 2:1). God never left him hanging on hope. He did respond to his waiting prophet. 'Then the Lord replied: Write down the revelation and make it plain . . . so that a herald may run with it . . . Though it linger, wait for it; it will certainly come and will not delay.' (Habakkuk 2:2–3) Wait for God. Write down what you sense is coming from the Lord for the purpose of recollection, reflection and confirmation. He will speak and continue to speak to you and even call you to more waiting.

Secondly, God's presence is like his voice. Let the presence of the Lord draw near and his voice is not far away. He always invites us to the burning bushes, the upper rooms of life and the valleys of decision. He has a way of getting us alone with him. His presence will actually draw you into the courts of the Lord. This is the classic stance of the prophets of old. As the three heavenly visitors left Abraham on their way to destroy the wicked city of Sodom, Genesis 18:22 includes this pregnant statement: 'But Abraham remained standing before the Lord.' The NIV Bible and the NIV Study Bible text note suggest an ancient scribal translation renders the verse: 'But the Lord remained standing before Abraham.' Both translations seem equally acceptable. It also provides a wonderful illustration of the mutual accessibility that existed between God and his prophet, or shall we say, God and his people.

Prayer and prophecy are inextricably tied together. One who intercedes gets an audience with God, and one who hears revelations from God will often be found in the place of prayer. But it is the God of Abraham, our God, who stands before us, seeking for us to come into his courts. To Isaiah he asked, 'Whom shall I send? And who will go for us?' (Isaiah 6:8). To the false prophets who tormented Jeremiah God asks, 'But which of them has stood in the council of the Lord to see or to hear his word? Who has listened and heard his word?' (Jeremiah 23:18). Listen to the cry of a disconnected prophet called Job: 'Oh, for the days when I was in my prime, when God's intimate friendship blessed my house' (Job 29:4). A literal translation of the end of the verse reads like this: 'When God's council was in my tent,' or, 'When God was intimate in my tent' (Job 29:4, NIV Study Bible text note). Just like Abraham, who stood before the Lord and spoke with him, so Job cries out for a return of that mutual highway of communication.

To the prophet Amos the Lord reveals his commitment to prophetic revelation in the performing of his will and states that he 'does *nothing* without revealing his plans to his servants the prophets' (Amos 3:7, my italics). The Hebrew word for 'council' is translated here with the word 'plans' (Jeremiah 23:18, NIV Study Bible text note). In a universal sense, we, the body of Christ, are called into the Lord's chambers to hear, see and receive God's battle plans for our own lives and the world. From that place before the Lord we can respond with Amos and say, 'The lion has roared—who will not fear? The Sovereign Lord has spoken—who can but prophesy?' (Amos 3:8).

Finally, in our quest of God's voice, we must learn to be a worshipper. We must emulate Mary at Jesus' feet. Instead of rushing about the house preparing meals, she chose to minister to Jesus' heart. She sat gazing into his lovely face. Worshippers get to hear the master's voice.

Consider the prophet Elisha. He was in a difficult position before King Jehoshaphat of Judah. He needed to hear from God so he requested, 'Bring me a harpist' (2 Kings 3:14–16). It was difficult getting a word from God because of Joram, the ungodly king of Israel. He just happened to be standing nearby watching the proceedings. Only worship that had heart in it and a heavenly voice could help Elisha. 'While the harpist was playing, the hand of the Lord came upon Elisha' and he received God's message (2 Kings 3:15).

Play worship music. Better still, worship on an instrument or with your voice, sing to him and he will talk back. There is no magic to the gift of prophecy. We all have to start at the feet of Jesus. Once his voice is heard, the door is wide open for his power to be released.

3

THE GIFT OF PROPHECY

Pierrette came rushing up to the front of the church at the Toronto Airport Christian Fellowship. She had recognised me from the platform and she was certainly not going to miss speaking with me. My eleven years as a Baptist pastor had taken me to various parts of Canada, and during one of those pastorates, Pierrette was a parishioner. 'Jim, do you remember me from Castor Valley Baptist Church?' she asked. 'You prophesied over my new-born baby.'

I've prayed for hundreds of people. It's hard to remember every face and prophecy. Yet I couldn't forget Pierrette and Trevor Wilson. Neither could I forget little Annik, the recipient of one of my first attempts at prophecy. I distinctly remember going to the hospital and speaking God's heart to this mother and new baby. Was I wrong? Did I really miss the mark? I've had to apologise before: was this another adventure in humility? All these thoughts raced through my mind. Just as I was thinking the worst, Pierrette announced, 'Oh Jim, everything you prophesied has come true!' I sighed with relief. It transpired that this baby has indeed been a special blessing to her family. She does have a beautiful voice and has been singing for the Lord in church. These were all words of prophecy that I had spoken over Annik some fourteen years ago.

My early attempts at hearing God and sharing his heart were for the most part successful. We've come to learn that faith is spelled RISK. The gift of prophecy is real and it has blessed many people during these days of renewal. But we all have to begin somewhere.

God's plan of the ages

We are living in days of answered prayer. Moses' prayer, uttered 3,500 years ago and recorded in Numbers 11:29—'I wish that all the Lord's people were prophets and that the Lord would put his Spirit on them'—is being fulfilled today. In North America, Europe and Asia, hundreds of believers are receiving the gift of prophecy as they are immersed in the presence and power of God's Spirit. There will always be the Joshuas in the camp who jealously want to keep the anointing for Moses, the 'Man of God'. However, when the glory of God came to the assembly and the Holy Spirit fell upon them even the elders Eldad and Medad, who were absent from the meeting, prophesied. God wants a 'prophetic Church'.

We are also living in the days of fulfilled prophecy—a 2,700-year-old prophecy! Down through the course of history, Joel saw a time when a revolutionary outpouring would come: 'And afterwards, I will pour out my Spirit on all people. Your sons and daughters will prophesy, your old men will dream dreams, your young men will see visions. Even on my servants, both men and women, I will pour out my Spirit in those days' (Joel 2:28–29).

On the day of Pentecost the Holy Spirit fell on the believers (Acts 2) and the book of Acts takes the next twenty-six chapters to record the unending river of revelation.

However, this was only a partial fulfilment of that Old Testament promise. Joel's prophecy described a Messianic age of the Spirit. Beyond the days of the apostles, beyond the days of the Reformation, God's Spirit would continue to flow throughout Church history until the consummation of all things.

Interestingly enough, Billy Graham has called the twentieth century the century of the Holy Spirit. As we come to the end of this century, the wind of the Spirit is blowing afresh and we are compelled to declare the King's agenda.

God has many ways of speaking

The prophetic gift that is often seen in our small groups, church services and renewal meetings has come in various forms. God has many ways of speaking to us and through us. John Sandford's book *The Elijah Task* sets out foundational teaching on the five ways God speaks.

Numbers 12:1–8 lists five ways God speaks to men. These are in a continuum, from the most indirect to the most direct. The most indirect way, which involves the least interference from the conscious mind, is through a dream. The second is by vision. There are three types of visions: a trance, in which the mind is nearly totally arrested; a picture flashed upon our inner screen while we are totally alert; or a direct seeing into the world of the spirit. Whatever the type, our minds are active and participating but the Holy Spirit is in charge and shows us the picture . . . the third way is by dark speech. In dark speech God uses language figuratively . . . The fourth step up the ladder is direct speech. We still hear this within our spirits, but God is speaking clearly to our minds, there are no puns or parables . . . Finally, the fifth way is the most clear. He speaks audibly.[9]

It's important to note that the 'pictures flashed on the inner screen' could be called 'words of knowledge' from the Spirit and can become words of prophecy when verbalised. Dr Jack Deere teaches that the gifts of word of knowledge and word of wisdom are actually sub-sections in the overall gift of prophecy.[10]

There is also the kind of prophecy that comes by 'impression'. You just know in your spirit that the Holy Spirit has deposited his wisdom or knowledge about a situation. It doesn't come as a 'picture' or as a 'still small voice'. You just know that God has spoken to you. I believe the apostle Paul's experience during his second missionary journey in Acts 16:6–10 suggests that he had an 'impression' from the Spirit of God. He had just finished seeing revival come to many of the cities of Asia Minor and it was natural to want to move on to Asia itself. However, he was 'kept by the Holy Spirit from preaching the word in the province of Asia' (6, KJV). They again tried to enter by way of Bithynia and again the 'Spirit of Jesus forbade them to enter' (7, KJV). It doesn't say that he had a word of knowledge or a pro-phecy from someone—simply that he was 'forbidden' by the Spirit of God to enter that new land. Strong impres-sions from the Spirit of God were nothing new to Paul and he had to hole up in the dingy port city of Troas, waiting for new directions from head office. They came in the form of the now famous night vision of the man from Macedonia calling out for help. The Holy Spirit directed the battle plans for the early Church. Why can't he be trusted to do the same in this generation?

Many of our ministry team have experienced these 'impressions' of the Spirit as they have prayed over people from around the world. One day I was praying for a man who said he felt nothing from God. As I prayed, I sensed that he was a computer engineer and he was approaching God in the same way! When I shared this thought he laughed and asked, 'How did you know?' Quickly, the floor came up to meet him and this computer Christian was overcome with passion for God.

When you get an 'impression', a 'word' or a 'picture' for someone while praying, it really is a prophetic gift that is operating through you by the Spirit. The whole area of the scriptural basis for the gift of prophecy will be discussed later in the book. But for now just be assured that you have at times been hearing from God even if it has come by means of 'impressions'.

Lightning rods

The same holds true during a worship service. A vision bursts in on your sight of chariots of fire or the sword of the Lord and you are caught up with him. It doesn't become a prophetic word until you share it with the church. However, when the vision is described it's like fire from heaven as the Holy Spirit releases his voice in the assembly. Only then does it become God's voice to his people as an interpretation is given. Often the first to speak are those whom we affectionately call the 'lightning rods'—those saints who feel the Spirit's presence quickly.

We'll never forget our first few visitors in May 1994 from Holy Trinity Brompton Anglican Church in central London. The height of British society, or so we thought.

Who said the British were reserved? When a secretary on the staff at HTB was touched by the power of the Spirit, she became our 'lightning rod' for the evening. Our British guest exploded with one-line prophetic prayers throughout John Arnott's sermon punctuating each point with precision. 'Oh, Je-sus!' she shouted as her voice vibrated in the steel rafters of the warehouse church. The effect was dynamic on the five hundred or so in attendance. It felt like Isaiah 64:1—God was indeed rending the heavens and coming down in our midst. As I remember, prayer for the faithful during the ministry time that evening was especially powerful.

One night while I was preaching, another 'Brit' was strategically positioned behind me on the platform in a horizontal position. During the sermon he too would shout out prophetic oracles, just when I was coming to the highpoint of my message: 'One, two, three, four, who are we fighting for . . . Jesus!' he proclaimed. Again, the service was charged with a passion for Jesus that infected us all.

Power encounter prophecies

There are also what we call shaking or ecstatic prophecies. These differ from prophecies spoken in the normal flow of a worship service. They are like power encounters with the almighty. It does not make a prophetic word any more valid if one shakes or not. It is simply a different administration of the gift (1 Corinthians 12:7). Yehezkel Kaufmann, in his book *The Religion of Israel*, suggests that ecstatic or shaking prophecy is consequent on the word of God; that is, in the Hebrew conception, ecstasy does not induce prophecy, as the pagans believed (ie the prophets of Baal on Mount Carmel, 1 Kings 18:28), but on the contrary, the divine word of God may cause ecstasy.[11]

Wes and Stacy Campbell, pastors from New Life Vineyard Christian Fellowship, Kelowna, British Colombia, are no strangers to powerful visitations of God's dynamic word. In 1988 the Holy Spirit descended upon their quiet Baptist church and all heaven broke loose prophetically. When they came to our church in autumn 1993, Stacy prophesied with a violent shaking of the head and body. We had never seen anything like that before. Once when Stacy was prophesying, I recall whispering a silent prayer, 'Oh Lord, please give me anything in your kingdom but that!' God didn't listen to me, as you will hear. Acts 2:2 does say that the Holy Spirit came into the upper room 'like the blowing of a *violent* wind from heaven' (KJV). The prophetic word Stacy gave was about God's Spirit coming to visit us in a new way and that our church would be a blessing to many.

After the Holy Spirit did indeed come in power in January 1994, the Campbells came back within a few weeks of the outpouring and held a special Saturday session with the congregation. Crucial teaching on renewal and the gift of prophecy was given, followed by a time of ministry. What 'glorious disorder' took place, as Charles Haddon Spurgeon so aptly described times of revival.[12] They asked for a prophetic impartation to come and the room exploded with believers shaking violently, some falling, some with arms gyrating, some doubled over. These were our own church people, basically godly believers not prone to wild emotional displays. When the prophetic words started to flow, I was relieved. It was as if the physical body went into overload as the word of the Lord came upon them!

Jeremiah understood the power of a prophetic word

encased in a mortal body as he said, 'His word is in my heart like a fire, a fire shut up in my bones. I am weary of holding it in; indeed, I cannot' (Jeremiah 20:9). There is definite power exerted through receiving holy words from the Lord. Jeremiah goes on to say, 'My heart is broken within me; all my bones tremble. I am like a drunken man, like a man overcome by wine, because of the Lord and his holy words' (Jeremiah 23:9). When one is plugged into God and his vast resources, it's no wonder we shake.

A spiritual tornado

I speak from experience when I say that I, too, have become a 'fool for Christ' (1 Corinthians 4:10). That's the statement of the hour for the Church. I don't have all the answers as to why someone shakes so violently. One thing I do know is that 'God opposes the proud but gives grace to the humble' (James 4:6). He is humbling his Church before a watching world.

On one occasion I was in a ministers' meeting, discussing the so-called 'Toronto blessing', and some dissension arose. While standing on the platform with the meeting chairman, I began visibly to vibrate. The team that had come with me from Toronto didn't know what was happening to me. All I knew was that the Lord's heart was broken over the rancour and I felt it deeply. He also gave me a verse from Scripture: 'As [Jesus] approached Jerusalem and saw the city, he wept over it' (Luke 19:41).

Like Jeremiah's encounter with God's word locked up in his heart, my bones were also on fire. The chairman turned to me in frustration and asked me to make some comment that would resolve the division. After quoting the verse, I exploded into a spirtual tornado. My arms flew from side to side and my head thrashed back and forth as these words came: 'You have no right to speak this way. You have not wept over this city. Come weep with me,' said the Lord. With that, I was thrown backwards in a circular motion and landed prostrate on the floor in absolute spiritual agony.

Never before had I wept so loudly as I responded to the Lord's word in my heart. It all took place before some of the most respected pastors of the city, but the Holy Spirit didn't seem to mind. Consequently, many pastors fell to their knees; some prayed, some groaned and some also began to prophesy. One pastor exclaimed, 'Don't you know that even today I can save men from the gutter and raise them to take your place?' Love for the lost, and unity of spirit, are high priorities for the Lord of the Church. The services that followed this outpouring were marked by many conversions and prodigals returning to the Lord.

Who said that the Holy Spirit was a gentleman? Ask King Saul. We read in 1 Samuel 10:5–7 that at the beginning the Spirit of the Lord came upon Saul in power and he began prophesying among a procession of prophets in the town of Gibeah, just as Samuel had said. But the next time he prophesied he was apprehended by the Holy Spirit. Some years later, as recounted in 1 Samuel 19:18–23, after Saul's anger against David became insatiable, he again prophesied but this time against his will. He had actually sent three different groups of soldiers to capture David, but they all were overcome by the Spirit of God and began to prophesy with the prophets of Naioth. You could just hear Saul muttering in his palace, 'If you're going to get anything done right, you've got to do it yourself!' so he went to Naioth to capture and probably kill David. Not a chance. The Spirit of God came even upon him, as he walked along the road, and he prophesied without clothes on his back, having stripped them off.

Ask Paul about his Damascus Road experience (Acts 8). Ask Ananias or Sapphira if the Holy Spirit is a gentleman (Acts 5). Not in the least. There are seasons in the life of the Church when he shows himself strong and he doesn't ask permission. God's purposes must be accomplished and we, as a result, come under his strong influence.

All the same rules of judging prophecy, as set out in 1 Corinthians 14, apply to any utterances, whether spoken in a shaking or stationary manner. They are just different operations of the same gift. But we cannot afford to condemn. We will see later, in the review of the historical record, that God did speak through these strong ecstatic prophecies, not to mention the manifestation of visions and trances to which we now turn.

4

VISIONS AND TRANCES

During renewal services in the city of Tainan, Taiwan on 16 June 1995, an amazing event took place. Grace Peng, a little eight-year-old girl was crying in her father's arms and I simply prayed that angels would come and comfort her and her family. 'Carpet time' soon flowed as Grace and her father rested in the Spirit. It was obvious that her fears had been relieved. Not long after, perhaps ten minutes or so, Grace's father came running to me in the church building, shouting, 'Come quick, my daughter is seeing Jesus!' I ran with him to the front of the church, near the altar. There she was weeping, tapping the floor and shouting in Mandarin Chinese, 'Jesus is standing right there, Jesus is there!' Grace was pointing to an open area of carpet at the front. No one could apparently stand on that spot of 'holy ground'. The power of God that one felt at that location was undeniable.

Face to face with Jesus

This phenomenon has been identified by Wes Campbell as an 'epicentre' of God's power,[13] a location in a building or city where people are overcome with a sense of God's presence. Could it be that the 'holy ground' is due to the presence of Jesus, the Holy Spirit or even angels? Moses was compelled to remove his shoes as he approached God's manifest presence at the burning bush (Exodus 3:1–6). Saul and the three separate bands of soldiers just approached Naioth in Ramah, where Samuel and the school of the prophets resided, and they were apprehended on God's 'holy ground.'

That evening in Taiwan we too were apprehended by God as this sweet little girl began to describe her open vision of Jesus. I encouraged her to gaze at his face and see his love for her, which she did. Slowly her eyes traced upwards and then stopped at about the height of a person's head. 'Look at his face of Love,' I urged Grace through an interpreter. Peace soon flooded upon her as almost everyone in the building was now watching Grace watching Jesus.

The power of the encounter galvanised all those in the service. Earlier, Grace's older sister had seen a shaft of light come down at that place on the floor and now she knew why. Jesus had entered the meeting in a dramatic way. He did say that 'where two or three come together in my name, there am I with them' (Matthew 18:20).

In short bursts Grace cried out, 'He is the ruler . . . He is the ruler. . . .' Spontaneous, en-masse repentance and groaning began taking place all around the hall. At that point she described the Lord as 'breathing on the congregation, blowing sin away'. Many angels were also identified as being in the room and ministering to those gathered there. An awesome event to say the least. Finally, the meeting was shaken as a prophetic release swept through the room. Many people began to have visions and prophetic utterances regarding a coming revival in Taiwan. 'Come Holy Spirit' meant something to our understanding of the literal presence of Jesus. Grace's life was transformed that night: no longer a frightened little girl, she was developing into a prayer warrior.

What happened to Grace was inspiring and heaven sent, yet she was able to remain lucid throughout her encounter. However, at times a vision is so intense that our bodies seem inert externally, but very alive to the heavenly kingdom. Don't forget that Daniel fell into a deep sleep when a vision of the Lord appeared (Daniel 8:17–18). John also had a similar experience on the island of Patmos. He was in the Spirit on the Lord's day when he came face to face with the sovereign Lord of history, and as a result fell at his feet as though he were dead (Revelation 1:9–10, 17–18).

Visions and trances are another way in which God speaks to us. Once described and interpreted for the listener, they take the force of a prophetic word. Whole books of the Bible such as Ezekiel, Daniel, Zechariah, Amos and Revelation are filled with visions that became God's voice to us. It's been my experience during this present move of the Spirit that visions often involve seeing spiritual events—heaven, hell, the 'harvest' at the end of time, angels, Jesus or future events. Trances seem to include all of the above, but intensified.

Our encounter with God and his kingdom can, if strong enough, overcome our frail human body and we get locked away with him in the vision. When the senses get locked up in this fashion, it's called a trance. The person often goes into a catatonic state as the scene unfolds before them or as they hear the divine dialogue.

Now my wife has accused me of similar manifestations when we go shopping. The most common appearance of the 'blank stare' comes when we attempt to discuss family affairs while I am watching sports on the television. Let's call it daydreaming or ADS—'Acquired Deafness Syndrome'. Many husbands suffer from this type of immobility. This is not the manifestation to which I am referring.

For a real example of prophetic vision, consider Amos, an Old Testament prophet, who was actually a farmer in the land of Judah. He had no great pedigree nor prophetic lineage, but he was inextricably joined to the creator. You don't need to be some great Christian mystic to be prophetically used by God. Just get connected to the Spirit of life.

The book of prophecy that bears his name in the Bible begins like this, 'The words of Amos, one of the shepherds of Tekoa—what he *saw* concerning Israel' (Amos 1:1, my italics). This vision was, as he said, the basis of his prophetic oracle. Visions of locusts (7:1), fire (7:4), a plumb-line (7:7), a basket of ripe fruit (8:1–6) and even the Lord himself standing by the altar (9:1) were the foundation for the 'word of the Lord' to be spoken. God often speaks to us in language and symbols that come from our own frame of reference. Amos was a farmer/shepherd so he spoke to him in imagery that was charged with meaning. God will do the same with you.

The best way to describe this grace of the Holy Spirit is to recount what we have seen taking place in the lives of believers. Visions have become the pictorial basis of life-giving words to the Church. Apparently spontaneously, the rain of God descends on a congregation and visions or trances take place. At times, in a conference setting, I will teach on 'prophecy in practice' and ask God for an outpouring. With little notice, 'kaboom'—a prophetic explosion descends. Occasionally, during a renewal meeting, the Lord will urge me to ask him for a revelatory release in the church, and again visions come to God's people. All of God's people, young and old and in between are hearing God in this fashion.

A love story

Have you ever tried to get young people to be quiet? Sometimes it can be impossible, at the best of times. Yet when the Holy Spirit comes with power there is life-changing silence.

At the March 1995 'Catch the Fire' conference in Thunder Bay, Ontario something happened to seventeen year old, Steven Karhunen. He indeed was 'in the Spirit' and came forward for prayer with the other 800 in the banquet hall. I had preached a simple, biblical message and Steve was one of the first to receive ministry. The following event took place. I will let Steve tell you his own life-changing story.

'It was the Saturday night renewal meeting in the Valhalla Inn—I was extremely depressed and heartbroken. I received ministry from Pastor Jim Paul and that night he prayed for me about the 'question mark' in my future. I fell under the power and was filled with peace.

'But I knew something was still missing. So my aunt and her friend prayed for me. I fell again and suddenly as I hit the floor my eyes shot wide open. They were open for one hour. I didn't blink once and my pupils were dilated (so I was told). During that time it felt as if I were in a trance. I was unaware of my surroundings and the people around me. I saw Jesus take from my body my heart, which was broken and torn apart. He replaced it with a bright-red, bigger heart.

'Then I saw a light. In that light I saw a head. Putting my hand up to cover myself from the light I saw the most beautiful human face I've ever seen. It was the face of Jesus. For about the next 45 minutes I lay there looking and smiling at him. He smiled back! It was the most intimate time of my life with someone. I fell deeply in love with him and all the heartbrokeness was gone. The next day as I testified to what happened, Pastor Jim Paul told me that my future was to be in Jesus' ministry. Many times I still see Jesus' face and I adore his love and beauty. I thank God for changing my life forever, for meeting me face to face and giving me a vision for my future.'

At the next service Steve was asked to testify about his wide-eyed experience. Encounters such as this must be put into shoe leather, so we asked him what change he felt took place in the realm of his heart. He explained about the absolute love that had come into his life after seeing Jesus. Then, right there on the platform, an instant replay took place. His eyes went off into the distance, gazing at some matchless beauty. He was again seeing Jesus. It was impossible for him to stand erect, so we helped him to the floor. At the mere mention of Jesus' name, this young man was swept into God's presence. This is not some charismatic fringe experience. The power of the Holy Spirit often brings a revelatory release that is life-transforming.

The king of Windsor Castle

Visions are awesome and dynamic but how would you or your church integrate them into everyday life? Testing their veracity through Scripture and waiting on God for more information are two key elements. But what does one do with visions after they are established as a real word from God?

This next story I will share with you describes how a pastor named Andy Lancaster and his congregation, King's Church in Windsor, verified and then applied God's vision. I heard this story while preaching in England. To give you some background, Windsor is a relatively small town in England, yet it is one of the most internationally renowned in the world. Thousands of tourists come each year to see Windsor Castle, which is one of the official residences of the monarch. You cannot help but be impressed with the scale of the castle which stands on the hill, almost dwarfing the town of some 30,000 inhabitants.

Over the past few years some amazing events have taken place in Windsor—natural events that could have direct spiritual parallels. In 1992, fire raged through part of the castle and dramatic pictures were broadcast around the world as teams of firemen fought to save the building from becoming totally consumed. Then, in 1993 a part of the town experienced flash floods, which in less than an hour left some streets waist deep in water. Finally, in 1994, there was astonishment when it was announced that exploratory drilling was being considered when engineers suggested the possibility of an untapped oil supply lying hidden under the castle!

This series of events could have been a coincidence, yet it seemed unusual for them all to happen in one relatively small town. The local spiritual leadership took notice of the signs of fire, water and oil in town, and began praying with even greater fervour for a move of God in Windsor. In a Chinese restaurant, in the shadow of Windsor Castle, I heard first hand of Andy's encounter with God. This is how his meeting with the Lord unfolded.

In October 1994, Andy came to visit the Toronto Airport Christian Fellowship with the other leaders who form part of the ministry team of King's Church in Slough and Windsor. They, along with many others, queued for hours ahead of the service and then squeezed into the original Dixie Road building, hungry for a fresh touch from God. During one of those ministry times Andy had what I can only describe as a vision from God about the town of

Windsor. It was not just a vague mental picture, but a real and vivid image that gripped his attention.

Andy saw himself kneeling by the wall of Windsor Castle banging on it with his fist, crying out for a move of God in the town. Given the resistance of the wall before him, the task seemed almost impossible. As the scene evolved, he noticed that his fist was bleeding from the constant blows against the wall.

'It was then,' Andy recounts, 'that I looked up and it was as if the huge walls before me exploded. The impact felt so powerful that it knocked me to the ground and I lay there for some time completely dazed. When I came around I noticed that I had a piece of the wall in my hand and it was covered in blood. My first thought was that it was the blood from my own hand while trying to break through the wall. But then, as I looked up, I saw what appeared to be an enormous vision of a man who I assume was Jesus. The magnitude of his being was astounding, towering over the castle and town, and the brilliance around his being made it impossible to make out any of his features.'

At that point he heard a voice speaking to him. 'The blood of no man is sufficient to break through the strongholds before you. It is only my blood that is sufficient for this!' It was then that Andy realized that the blood which covered the stone in his hand was not his, but the blood of Jesus, shed on the cross.

Initially, he saw this vision as an encouragement to him because it had been quite hard going in the months leading up to his visit to Toronto. The team had been experiencing a number of battles and it was so good to get a renewed perspective before God. However, on returning to Windsor, the Holy Spirit brought another dimension to what had just been described.

Around the restaurant table that evening, more than chop sticks were shaking as this vision was retold. The impact of the encounter resonated within us. 'Would you like to go to the spot where I was kneeling in the vision'? Andy asked. 'It's not far from here.'

Somehow we managed to get out the door and make our own way down the pavement flanking the castle wall. A party of four paraded down the street: Wesley Richards, the senior leader at King's, Andy Lancaster with his wife Lu, and myself. I'll never forget the gasp uttered when we discovered a small cross at about eye level to someone who would be kneeling before the wall. I placed my finger around the detail of the cross and knew that it wasn't some hatchet job. It was purposely etched in stone with great care, marking someone's untimely death. Wesley recalled that it was a memorial to the death of a martyr. The vision took another significant step forward. We were immediately impacted by the power of the Holy Spirit as we viewed that memorial.

Some research into local history revealed that this mark was reported to have been placed on the wall during the reign of King Henry VIII as a memorial to a young man who was beheaded because he publicly criticised one of the king's unrighteous relationships. Further research confirmed the shedding of additional blood in the deaths of three Christian men known as the Windsor martyrs in the mid-1500s. They stood against the unrighteous 'establishment' in the town of the time, and were publicly executed.

More evidence was uncovered of the 'establishment' resistance that took place in 1875. On this occasion D.L. Moody was refused permission to hold an open-air meeting by the governing body of Eton College which is situated close to the castle. Such was the opposition that the matter was actually raised in the House of Lords. Fortunately, a local shopkeeper agreed to hold the event behind his shop which resulted in an open-air meeting of about a thousand people. This information brought great encouragement to Wesley and Andy because when King's Church, Windsor was first planted in 1987 they had received a word from Isaiah 60:22 which said: 'The least of you will become a thousand, the smallest a mighty nation. I am the Lord; in its time I will do this swiftly.'

As a result of the initial vision and the following revelation, they have now begun a church prayer walk and regularly circle the castle and town centre. This involves prayer that the kingdom of God will come in greater measure in the town and that the blood of Jesus will break the power of any unrighteous authority which might seek to oppose revival. 'We are also praying,' Andy notes, 'that even though the shed blood of the martyrs who stood against certain aspects of the unrighteous "establishment" in Windsor may not in itself be sufficient to break strongholds, it may truly be a seed for future revival.'

By way of conclusion, Andy confirms that 'without a doubt the vision which I received while at the Toronto Airport Christian Fellowship has not only been of great personal encouragement, but has also significantly sharpened our spiritual insight and intercession for Windsor.'

Let us now turn to those dark sayings that come to us in the form of dreams. Night visitations are not some poor sister to these more public prophetic manifestations. Every part of our humanity can receive God's voice, even our spirit that rests under his protection. The one who gives his beloved sleep is also the one who stays awake during the night, both to watch over us and to speak to us.

5

DREAMS

Have you ever been awakened by your spouse with an up-to-the-minute rendition of night visions—more commonly known as dreams? This is a constant occurrence in my house. Dianne, my wife of twenty-two years, admits that she doesn't get many prophetic words but she does receive prophetic dreams. These have increased in number and clarity as she has been anointed by the sweet presence of God.

Buildings and aeroplanes

One morning in the spring of 1994, I heard the account of a particularly vivid dream that my wife had just received during the night. It was significant, symbolic and difficult to interpret. Like Mary, we treasured all these things and pondered them in our hearts (Luke 2:19). At times that's all you can do until the Spirit of God releases a gift of interpretation.

The dream was in three parts, with the last two portions directly relating to Dianne's personal life. However, the first section seemed more global. It was a scene enacted in a massive building. At that time the Toronto Airport Fellowship was in a small industrial unit that could hardly fit the bill. In this dream, Dianne and I were standing in the midst of a huge building—almost like a conference centre with large posts and with many windows surrounding the hall. There were scores of people about us. Then, suddenly, several large pieces of an aeroplane began racing through the room at a frenetic speed. One after another, they ploughed through the audience. Surprisingly, however, no one was hurt. Abruptly, the dream passed on to another subject leaving my wife troubled by this very symbolic night vision.

It began to make sense during our first visit to the new church facility on Attwell Drive—the other side of Toronto Airport. It's at the departure section instead of the tail-end of the runway. Thank God the rumbling of jet engines are all but gone. Dianne had not seen this conference centre before, yet it occupied the same building she had seen in her dream several months ago. We knew that this almost cavernous building was God's gift to our church. We also knew that the 73,000 square feet of carpet would be full of people one day. That has already happened many times since the building was officially turned over to us on 20 January 1995—one year after God's Spirit was poured out upon us.

Pieces of an aeroplane dashing through the building was more difficult to interpret. Would there be a plane crash? Was the building under attack? Would there be an accident? All these ideas rushed through my mind. It wasn't until December 1995 when we shared this dream with Ian Ross, the associate pastor at the church, that we received God's perspective. Dreams were never meant to be left in the dark. The God of Daniel is in our midst—'God in heaven who reveals mysteries' (Daniel 2:28).

Ian suggested that the pieces of an aeroplane racing through that building represented this local church fellowship. 'A breaking process was to take place,' Ian said. 'It was symbolic of a period of humbling that has come to the Toronto Airport Fellowship. Just days before, we were told as a church to disengage from the Association of Vineyard Churches, basically because of the different model we used for the administration of the renewal. This was both sudden and painful. Indeed it felt like God was breaking and humbling us, just as if pieces of an aeroplane were flung into our church. However, both Dianne and I knew that we were to press ahead through our pain. We had been prepared by a prophetic dream.

A people of dreams

Dreams have been the basis of great blessing in the Church. In this time of renewal we should be looking for God to comfort, challenge and direct us during the night watches. 'He who watches over you will not slumber' (Psalm 121:3). He wants to communicate with you even in your sleep and bestow the blessing of revelation. Now, it must be stressed that not all dreams are from God. A bad meal, a quarrel with your spouse or a frightening film could be the source of wild nocturnal sights. We need to test them in the same way and with the same tenacity that prophecies are tested.

James Ryle has written a masterful book on the subject, *A Dream Come True*, in which he describes six ways to recognise false dreams and visions. The tests can be reduced to the following six questions. Are they seductive? Are they corrupt? Are they contradictory? Are they discouraging? Are they unproductive? Are they destructive? Simply put, do the dreams glorify God, lift up Jesus and are they in accordance with the teachings of Scripture?[14]

Saints throughout the ages have heard God speak to them in dreams and we are the benefactors of the decisions that flowed from these night revelations. Did you know that the Christian classic *Pilgrim's Progress*, written by John Bunyan in the seventeenth century, was inspired by a dream he received while in Bedford prison? How about that precious Christian hymn 'Amazing Grace', composed by John Newton, the eighteenth century slave trader turned radical Christian? This too was inspired by a dream.[15]

God's dream network

Chapter after chapter could be filled with dream stories of the newly anointed. Days of heaven have come upon us and we are receiving from the 'Father of lights' both day and night. Let me tell you one interesting encounter I had with a dreamer in Thailand.

The 'Catch the Fire' meetings that I attended in Bangkok, Thailand in June 1995 were unforgettable in many respects. First, I came to realise that God is sending the same visions to the earth, adapted to local cultures. One morning after teaching on the prophetic gift, a prophetic blessing descended upon the gathering of missionaries and leaders from the Thai nation. A vision of the 'Harvest' was the first to be described. It was exactly like the one we have heard in North America where the believer is ushered into a vast field of wheat, ready for a massive harvest—except it was a field of rice. It was essentially the same vision but a different cultural image.

Not only did God speak in the context of the Thai people but he also announced our visit through his dream network. Agnes Fellows, a Kenyan living in Thailand, received a stirring dream on the fifth night of our renewal meetings. Agnes had no information about the meetings yet God told her that there were four people coming to Thailand. In her dream, she saw clearly three men and a woman. She had no way of knowing that on my team there were four: Jimmy Dowds, Don Young, Carol Low and myself. Agnes described her dream as follows:

'The night of 28 June 1995 I had a dream. I saw three men and one lady. I simply asked who they were. Then there was a very strong light which shone in my direction. I could only see the light, but a voice began speaking to me. The voice was coming from the light and said, "There is a present I have brought to Thailand but I do not have enough people to give [it out]." Then the light and the voice disappeared.

'This light and voice returned twice more in the dream. I saw the same four people and the voice again said there was a gift for Thailand and that there were not enough people [to receive it]. Then I asked why there were not enough people and the voice from the light said that the inhabitants were Buddhists and they did not believe in him, neither worship him and that I was to give this message to the four people—the servants of God.'

What would you do if you were arrested by God's light and voice in your sleep? I, personally, would run to the meeting. After making some telephone calls to local churches, Agnes did just that. She came to the conference centre in Bangkok the next day and relayed this message—she could only obey. It was her turn to receive a blessing or 'present' as the Lord described it.

Furthermore, the message in Agnes's dream was quite

interesting. We were amazed that the Lord was announcing the 'blessing' in new ways, beyond our wildest imaginations. He was using his dream network to direct the anointing. That dream resolved for me the purpose of this preaching mission. We were clearly called by God to spread the fire and preach the gospel in Buddhist Thailand.

Let's be honest. Thoughts of unworthiness can often assail our minds. Is this you, God? Do you really want me to leave my family for days on end? Will you actually refresh these Thai believers through preaching and ministry? Yet God was at the very centre of this ministry visit. We had a 'present' of the Holy Spirit to impart. Before the team left Thailand, we had the opportunity of holding several powerful renewal conferences in the cities of Chiang Mai (north), Tak (west) and Hat Yai (south). Agnes's dream had been fulfilled.

Not only has God been encouraging us and declaring his will to us through dreams, but he is also ministering to us through angelic visitations. The next chapter concerns some ordinary believers who have had some extraordinary encounters. The hosts of heaven are among us!

6

ANGELIC VISITATIONS

Growing up in the Church, especially during the days of the 'Jesus People', angel sightings or rumours of sightings were a weekly event. Some encounters, however, were life changing.

Rumours of angels

My own Sunday school teacher in Hamilton, Ontario told us of his encounter with an angel that knocked on his door one snowy day. This was his story as I remember it. Early one morning, a little man stood on the front step urgently explaining to him the immediate danger the teacher's boys faced in their first-floor bedroom. He ran to verify the strange visitor's words only to find the curtains on fire right next to their bed. Smoke was everywhere inside the house and he fought madly to put out the flames. The window was closed and, as a result, no trace of smoke could have warned a neighbour or pedestrian. Once the fire was extinguished and the boys were safe, the Sunday school teacher went back to thank the stranger. No one was there! Not even a trace of footprints could be found in the morning snow. Intriguing indeed for our teacher and a classroom full of junior high students. That morning in church, I gained a new understanding of God's mercy through a first-hand account of an angel in our midst.

Angelic visitations have graced the Church since Gabriel visited Mary in Luke 1:26-38, not to mention the Old Testament encounters. Their appearances come like beacons on the road of Church history, often marking turning points in the life of the world at large or even a single believer. Before Sodom and Gomorrah felt the fire of God, angels came to warn and deliver (Genesis 18, 19). Before Jesus our Saviour was born, many angels at different times and settings came to prepare the way. Even now there is a noticeable increase of visitations from 'God's flaming messengers' (Hebrews 1:7). This seems to be taking place as the Church embraces a fresh outpouring of heaven and the possible consummation of all things. Now, when the angel Gabriel visited Mary she had every good reason to be 'greatly troubled', even 'afraid' (Luke 1:39-30). At times our faculties go into overdrive as we come face to face with the presence of eternity.

The wave stopper

A notable sighting took place near the beginning of our own visitation of God's Spirit at our fellowship. I have shared this story around the world and it clarifies what I believe the Lord is doing with his Church.

Lucy Lafrance, one of our youth leaders, was feeling somewhat perplexed during one of our renewal services in April 1994. After sitting down in the front row of the church, she asked if I could help her understand an encounter she had just had with an angel. She then told me this story.

'I saw a huge wave like that of the ocean, rolling into the sanctuary. I knew that it was a wave of revival that was going to crash down over the front of the church. Then, all of a sudden, it stopped dead in its tracks. A large angel had appeared in front of the advancing wave and with the raising of his hands, the wave just stopped.'

Lucy was clearly unsettled. She didn't know why this angel would come at just that time and stop God's blessing. The Lord released to me, I believe, a gift of interpretation. I will discuss that whole subject in the next chapter on 'prophetic signs'. The Church on the whole, I explained, is being prepared for a massive revival. All we are receiving right now is the refreshing that comes from the crest of the waves that are breaking over the angel and falling on God's people. Lucy retorted quickly, 'Yes, that's it, that's it!'

The big angel had every good reason to be in church that evening. It's interesting that the 'times of refreshing' label has become a common name for church or city-wide renewal services. That's exactly what God is doing in his people, but soon the 'wave' of revival will come crashing down—God will tell his angelic servant to step aside.

Miracle makers

Another angelic appearance came to a young couple while driving through northern Minnesota. I met Andrew and Sue Polkki in their home in Thunder Bay, Ontario during a 'Catch the Fire' conference and distinctly remember praying for Andrew and confirming the call of God on his life for missions. The following story of their encounter with the hosts of heaven is indicative of God's mark on their lives and that the day of wonders has come to the Church. I will let Sue Polkki recount her own walk with the angels.

'On 11 May 1995, my husband (then, fiancé) Andrew and I decided to take a day trip to Duluth, Minnesota. We had some wedding items to purchase and since the wedding was only a couple of months away, we thought it a good time to go. We had a wonderful day and on the way back to Thunder Bay we were both relaxed and happy.

'About an hour before the border crossing into Canada, we switched seats and I got behind the wheel. I'd driven a lot during the night and was a bit paranoid about wildlife on the road. At approximately 11.10 pm a moose ran out onto the road, right in front of our car. We swept it off its feet and it landed with a big thud on our roof, taking out the windshield along with it. I didn't even have a chance to brake—we hit the moose at full speed. I hit the steering wheel and the whole roof caved in. At this point we were both unconscious, but I was totally confused and had no idea what had just happened. I just sat there with my foot on the brake whimpering. A short time later, Andrew's head cleared and he opened his door and climbed out. He came around to my side and pulled me out of the vehicle and laid me down on the side of the road and shortly afterwards came back to pray for me. By this time I was going in and out of consciousness. Andrew commanded God's healing into my body and prayed that I would see ministering angels because every time I came to, I was frightened. However, he knew without a doubt that I would be fine and felt an inner peace that kept him together, despite the fact that we were stranded late at night on a deserted road, deep in remote northern Minnesota.

'Probably within a minute from the time Andrew started praying for me, he looked up and saw a flashing light. The

vehicle turned out to be an ambulance that was transport-
ing a patient to Grand Marais (the nearest town). The
ambulance stopped and administered first aid to us and
brought us to the hospital in Grand Marais.

'I have no recollection of the moose, the accident, the
ambulance or the night in the hospital. I can recall only a
few things. After Andrew had laid me down on the side of
the road, I remember feeling a lot of pain and a fear that
consumed me. I opened my eyes to look for Andrew, but
instead I saw four angels gathered around me, speaking
love, comfort and peace to me. The angels were magnifi-
cent in beauty. They weren't white or shiny: I can only
describe them as glorious. They were speaking quietly to
me and one angel was kneeling by my side and I could see
that he had his hand inside my chest. He was working on
something. All I know is that he healed me.

'I still remember fearing for Andrew and I turned my
head to look for him and saw him walking towards me.
He had two angels with him too. Then I saw something
that disturbed me at that moment. I saw our car, and
sitting on the caved-in roof were about six more angels.
The angels didn't bother me, it was their actions that did.

'Unlike the other angels who were comforting us, these
just sat there, joking, carrying on and throwing their heads
back in laughter. It looked like they were having a big party
on the top of our smashed car. I thought, 'How can they
be so happy while I'm lying here, maybe dying!' I knew
they were here to save me but I was certainly puzzled.

'On arrival at the hospital, Andrew and I were checked
over for any major injuries and other than a few minor
issues, we were fine. By all rights we should have been
dead. I felt like asking, 'By whose right?' Obviously, God
still wanted us on this earth. The doctors had taken X-rays
of me, expecting to find broken bones and other injuries,

but the X-rays showed that I was intact. Even the break in my nose had been set by the time I reached the hospital.

'In the late morning of 23 May, I was released from the hospital and we went to see our car. By looking at it we knew that it was only through God's grace that we were alive and only suffered minor injuries. The roof was completely caved in except for one small area where Andrew's head had been. It looked like a helmet had been put there to protect his head. The side door which Andrew used to get out of the wreck was smashed. Angels must have opened that door too.

'We also found out about the story of the miraculous arrival of the ambulance. The patient in the vehicle had complained that the ambulance stalled shortly after picking him up. Then about a half hour later, it just started. Once on the road again they spotted us. Andrew and I were totally amazed.

'The miracles God performed during the accident were just astounding. For a long time I was still puzzled about the angels that were having such a good time on the car, until my mother-in-law added some insight. She told me that she could just imagine the angels stalling the ambulance and then gathering around afterwards on the roof of the car telling stories about how they delayed the ambulance. They probably found the whole thing very amusing. But, whatever the reason, I will never forget the sight of those angels.'

Ministers of fire

Britain has not been short of angelic visitations during this present renewal. While preaching in the North, I heard this first-hand report of the heavenly host attending a church service at the Woodgate Church in Birmingham.

After a regional renewal conference, Ranvir Sahota's story came to light. 'I had been aware of supernatural phenomena,' Ranvir confessed, 'but I spent most of my intellectual life trying to explain them away.' Interestingly, he was saved on the very Sunday he went to disrupt the service and beat up the pastor. He had a life-changing Damascus Road encounter with Jesus during the worship service, before he could get to the pastor. I'm sure that Sunday, pastor Mike Price was also rejoicing with the angels.

On Sunday 12 March 1995, Ranvir began to see many angels in the church. About twelve were arranged on the stage, singing and playing instruments during worship. One particular angel played a large, round, golden instrument. Afterwards, other angels appeared on stage, and one began drawing the smoke rising from the believers into himself (possibly the prayer incense mentioned in Revelation 5).

Another angel then began to throw fire balls at the congregation. When the balls landed on the individuals, the level of praise noticeably increased in the church. Others that were hit seemed to store the fire in their bodies. Ranvir also saw angels protecting the offering and the worship team. They even bared their swords during the time when prophetic words were given. Then one who appeared as the person of the Holy Spirit took the stage while Pastor Mike preached the word. All the other angels bowed before him as the vision drew to a close.

In conclusion to this memorable event, Ranvir reflected that 'such an encounter was nothing in comparison to the joy of worship'. A sobering remark, even in the face of supernatural phenomena. The pastoral staff commented that the service was unusually blessed by the Spirit that morning. Even spots on the stage were endued with power.

Hosts of heaven

Further north in Scotland, angels visited the 'Catch the Fire' conference in Edinburgh during the Easter weekend of April 1995. The grand old Usher Hall had more than believers filling the seats.

Andy Lamond of The Vine Fellowship in Dunfermline, Scotland witnessed the presence of ministering angels. During the worship he saw many angels coming down through the roof. Some were stationed by those who were shaking, others were protecting the spiritual climate of the building, making sure nothing evil could get in. The angels were also holding flaming swords and at one point when Carol Arnott was speaking about the white horse of the end times, he heard a trumpet blast. The sound was so distinct that he turned to his companion to see if he also heard the music. It was a call to arms! It was as if we were already in the battle and it was time to take our places and fight.

One of the angels then gave a blazing sword to Carol Arnott and indicated that she was to start using it. Possibly that meant that Carol was to have a new authority in communicating the word of God which the apostle Paul describes as the 'sword of the Spirit' (Ephesian 6:17). During that time I happened to be physically supporting Carol and I sensed the absolute presence of eternity. No wonder. The angels had come. Jesus did say that 'the harvest is the end of the age, and the harvesters are angels' (Matthew 13:39).

The prophetic Church of the last days will be a Church endued with the Spirit's power and enabled by the host of heaven. The host will also declare the word of the Lord both verbally and non-verbally. In the following study of prophetic signs we will investigate the whole phenomenon of 'pantomime' prophecies and revelatory 'signs' of the Holy Spirit in our midst.

7

PROPHETIC SIGNS

On Easter Sunday 1994, during our morning service, an interesting event took place. As the Spirit began to rest on those who came forward for prayer, Melanie, an eighteen-year-old leader in our youth group, fell to the floor. This was a normal occurrence for us at the Toronto Airport Christian Fellowship, but what was about to happen was new to us. Almost instantaneously, Melanie's hand became clenched like a fist and then came a strange action of the fist rocking back and forth. At first sight you would dismiss it as just the flexing of a sore hand or wrist, but this was not the case.

'Pantomine' prophecy

The Spirit was pantomiming, acting out in a visual form a word for the church. A gift of interpretation came to Melanie that this action was similar to the stone that once covered Jesus' grave. She then spoke out the stirring affirmation: 'I'm alive, I'm alive, don't treat me as though the rock still covers my grave.' Again we saw the value of waiting on God to explain what he is doing with our bodies. We are the only present-day tabernacle of the Holy Spirit.

In both the Old and New Testaments, prophets visually expressed God's word through symbolic acts or 'signs'. A similar unction of prophetic mime is being seen today, as the Spirit of prophecy falls on the Church.

Ezekiel, Jeremiah and Agabus all used pictorial 'signs' that were followed by an interpretation: 'This is that.' Twelve times Ezekiel was directed by God to act out a prophetic word with his own body. These are forms of prophetic mime, often using inanimate objects. Here are a number of examples from Ezekiel: 3:22,26—tied with ropes; 4:1–3—built a model of the city of Jerusalem under seige; 4:4–8—prophet laid on his side; 4:9–11—barley and beans eaten for 390 days; 4:12–14—cooked with excrement; 5:1–3—shaved his head; 12:1–16—dug through the wall; 12:17–20—trembled as he ate; 21:6–7—groan in public; 21:18–24—made two sign posts; 24:15–24—no grief at his wife's death; 37:15–28—two sticks joined together. One of Ezekiel's most notable actions was his lying on his left side for 390 days and then on his right side for 40 days (4:4–8); the 40 days was interpreted as the 40 years of wickedness in Israel.

In addition to the siege enactment, there was the troubling prophetic mime of cooking a vegetarian meal on a fire made of human excrement (4:12–17). God heard Ezekiel's impassioned plea and let him use cow dung instead! Simply put, the lesson is – learn to pray if you're going to act out God's word prophetically!

Jeremiah's seven-fold use of 'signs' are found in the following verses: Jeremiah 13:1–11 (hiding a linen belt); 16:1–4 (not allowed to marry and have children in Israel);

16:5–9 (not allowed to attend a funeral); 19:1–12 (breaking a jar in public); 27:1–22 (a yoke carried on the neck); 32:6–15 (buying a field) and 43:8–13 (hiding stones in Egypt). God was merciful to Jeremiah and the most awkward prophetic act he had to perform was hiding his linen belt (a euphemism for 'underwear') in a rock crevice (13:1–11).

There are also prophetic acts employed by New Testament prophets. In Acts 21:10–13 we see Agabus moved by the Holy Spirit to take the belt from Paul's waist and tie his own hands and feet. Subsequently, the interpretation came announcing Paul's impending arrest in Jerusalem.

Whether they are acted out or occur in a non-pictoral fashion, prophetic 'signs' will be troublesome or even misunderstood if there is no accompanying gift of interpretation. It's my understanding of Scripture that a sign plus interpretation equals prophecy. Take the gift of tongues which Paul calls 'a sign' in 1 Corinthians 14:22. Edification comes to the whole church when the public use of tongues is followed by interpretation. As a result, Paul equates that two-fold manifestation of the Spirit in 1 Corinthians 14:2–5 to prophecy. In effect, God's people are hearing God's heart in their own language.

The same principle of prophetic mime with interpretation has been evident in our recent experience with the Holy Spirit. Amazing actions and sounds have graced many meetings: groaning, jumping, arm windmilling, hand chopping, twirling, running, bending and boxing, just to mention a few. It's important that the pastors who are overseeing any meeting seek for an interpretation of the signs that may be employed.

End-time horses

Take, for example, Eleanor's stomping of the feet and then galloping around the stage at the Usher Hall in Edinburgh during one Sunday evening service in spring 1995. It was surprising. No words accompanied the actions, but the effect was decisive. 'I saw heaven standing open,' John states 'and there before me was a white horse, whose rider is called Faithful and True. The armies of heaven were following him, riding on white horses' (Revelation 19:11, 14).

This first occurred in my experience at the morning service at Edinburgh City Fellowship. A strong prophetic mantle fell on the church. John and Carol Arnott's simple invocation unleashed a plethora of prophetic signs and words. Eleanor testified to her church that morning what she sensed God was saying through her wild actions. In essence, she felt that God's angelic horsemen, that are coming to bring in the end-time harvest, were being prefigured by her actions (Matthew 13:39).

In June 1995 while I was in Bangkok, Thailand for a series of renewal meetings, this same prophetic mime was seen. It has helped us to see that God's Spirit is sovereignly speaking one similar message. 'He who has an ear, let him hear what the Spirit says to the churches' (Revelation 2:17). During one of the 'pastors' and 'leaders'' sessions, the spirit of prophecy fell on the 300 who were present. Visions and prophecies were quickly released to those who reposed in various positions on the floor. One young man experienced a strong shaking of his legs, like that of a horse about to race over the earth. He was initially frightened by the encounter and fought off the impulse. The next day during the time of testimony, I asked him what was happening to him and if he felt he had any interpretation from the Lord. He suggested to us at the conference that this visual word was about the impending arrival of the 'horses of God'.

He had never been to Scotland, nor had he seen that demonstration of prophetic mime, and yet, half way around the world the Spirit spoke to a separate culture with the same biblical imagery. Before the testimony was finished he obviously lost his fear and was galloping and neighing on the floor, acting out the approaching cavalry from heaven.

Interpreting the imagery makes all the difference. It would not have been wise to judge such an act on the spur of the moment and so to condemn the man as simply fooling around or even being demonised. Interview and testimony are crucial in this situation. Yet not every wild action is some cryptic 'word from God'. Church leaders need to consult with both God and the believer before either accepting or condeming the prophetic enactment. However, we have often found that these strange encounters are indeed prophecies in mime, born of the Spirit of God.

Visual signs

Air India flight number 181 lifted off from Heathrow Airport on 17 February 1995, and I quickly fell asleep in the aisle seat. After spreading the 'blessing' across England for ten days, this preacher had battle fatigue. My study books were safely stowed in the empty seat beside me and I was dreaming of home, when all of a sudden a baby dropped on my head! Yes, a real live baby with all the fixings landed on my unprotected head and bounced onto my lap. Beside me stood an old man who scooped the baby out of my lap and fled to the back of the plane.

Briefly viewing the scene, I knew exactly what had transpired. This baby had been fussing with his young mother a few rows ahead of me and an older man, presumably her father, had come up to help her. During that attempt, the baby was dropped right on top of my head. Some help he was! I now had a bruise on my face for the journey. People seated around me looked for my reaction. Will he scream? Will he complain to the airline representative? Will he go to another seat? Not at all! I didn't respond negatively, because the voice of the Holy Spirit alerted me that this was a prophetic sign.

The Holy Spirit said to me: 'Just as this baby was struggling in the arms of his grandfather, so also there is a whole wave of spiritual babies struggling to get free of their traditions, and I will let them fall "suddenly" into the lap of my Church. They will leave their old ways and religions behind and will be swept into the body of Christ. This will be a sudden act. I will wake up my Church. It has been sleeping. It's not because of the absolute holiness of my Church that I will bring this revival, this people movement. It is because of my absolute love for those who are about to fall to the ground.'

I have had some interesting times on aeroplanes. On my way to Scotland in October 1994, I was punched in the head by a youth seated behind me. All of a sudden he didn't like me! Interestingly, within a few days several college students were also kicked and punched on their way to one of the 'Times of Refreshing' meetings being held in downtown Edinburgh. I had been forearmed with the comfort of God and the word of God for these bruised boys: 'Satan has been flushed into the light and he cannot stop the Spirit of the living God.' I've seen a businessman start shaking in the seat next to me after I had shared the gospel and prayed with him. One man on a recent flight even got drunk sitting right next to me. No, it wasn't the complimentary beverages. It was a 'peanuts and coke run'. My wife was shocked as she viewed the proceedings and asked me what I had done. 'Oh, I've been praying for him during the flight while touching him with my elbow,' I explained. God will give us 'signs' of his presence even on aeroplanes!

Prophetic signs are markers from heaven that we are on the threshold of a divine breakthrough. In a recent edition of *Ministries Today*, Jack Hayford, the senior pastor of the The Church of the Way, makes several helpful comments about the present-day 'signs' in our midst.

> 'Signs' are never the substance of something God is doing – they are just signposts pointing to what God is doing or about to do. So today's unusual manifestations of laughter, falling and roaring ought not to be responded to with criticism too quickly. Rather, we should be open to accept what may be a holy alert . . . The present multiplication of strange, bewildering activities does have an amply justifiable proof-text found in Acts 2: 19–20 'I will show wonders in the heaven above and signs on the earth below, blood and fire and billows of smoke. The sun will be turned to darkness and the moon to blood before the coming of the great and glorious day of the Lord.' That's a text applicable to any season during these post-Pentecost 'last days' of divine visitation. We are wise to expect wonders and signs in advance of any occasion on which God may visit us with his saving blessings and quick judgment on evil's dark powers.[16]

I would have chalked up this experience of a baby falling into my lap as just another hazard of flying, but the Lord said that it was a sign of a coming people movement. I've been convinced by the Lord to believe that a 'harvest' is falling into the lap of the Church. Spiritual babies are on the way!

Do you believe that the world is going to hell in a hand basket? Are you convinced that the Church will just prevail until the end and then be whisked away from an angry earth that, *en masse*, refused the gospel? I don't believe so! There is enough scriptual evidence for me to believe that the nations will come to Jesus, let alone the overriding evidence of world revival and 'harvest' that presently exists in the Third World. Just look at the conversion rates in the Far East, Africa and South America and you should be convinced that the gospel has not lost its power.[17]

Scripture speaks openly of 'the knowledge of the glory of the Lord' filling the earth 'as the waters cover the sea' (Habakkuk 2:14). The 'knowledge' spoken of there is not some intellectual assent, but rather the word used when Isaac went into the marriage tent and 'knew' his wife Rebekah (Genesis 24:67). The whole earth will be filled with his glory and many scores of people will intimately 'know' the Lord. How about Psalms 2:8 where we listen into a dialogue between God and his Son, the Messiah: 'Ask of me, and I will make the nations your inheritance.' Jesus our Messiah responded with a resounding 'yes' and 'asked' for the nations to be his portion. Have you considered Isaiah 53:11? Here the promise to the Messiah is this: 'After the suffering of his soul, he will see the light of life and be satisfied.' The cross did it all! Jesus will be completely satisfied as his blood will cover nations and peoples of every tribe and tongue as they respond to the gospel. 'This gospel of the kingdom will be preached in the whole world as a testimony to all nations, and then the end will come' (Matthew 24:14).

We've been hearing this same message, time and again, from many quarters of the Church. How long will we have to wait? John Dawson, in his recent book *Healing America's Wounds*, also contemplates this long-expected harvest in similar terms of babies and birthing. Why would God delay the arrival of the child of promise? John thinks it is because the size of the baby determines the length of a pregnancy. Consider the gestation period of an elephant – twenty to twenty-two months, as opposed to that of a field mouse – eighteen to twenty-one days.[18]

We don't want a mouse revival, we want an elephant revival – one that covers the earth with God's glory. There is a 'big baby' about to fall into the arms of the body of Christ. God is encouraging his Church through 'prophetic signs' that it takes time. Could it be, however, that the baby of revival is about to arrive on the scene? Signs from heaven have been coming in many different forms. Not only have babies been falling on our laps, but there has also been fire falling from heaven and the sound of the shophar (the ram's horn) declaring a last-days shaking of evil.

As the Holy Spirit falls on the Church, so his influence increases in the wider world. Peter clearly stated in his sermon at Pentecost that a day was coming when the Lord 'will show wonders in the heaven above and signs on the earth below' (Acts 2:19). In the greater context of the outpoured Spirit, a prophetic river came to many of the people of God. There is also the added dimension of cosmic signs and occurrences that cause the nations to wonder. The net result is that people will 'call on the name of the Lord' (Acts 2:21). One of the obligations of being a 'prophetic Church' in these crucial days is that we should allow God to make us his conduits for the miraculous, the revelatory.

Fire-balls from heaven

While preaching at the June 1995 'Catch the Fire' conference in Bangkok, Thailand, I met two of these precious, Holy Spirit 'conduits'—Sophal and Deborah Ung, native Cambodian pastors who are now planting churches in the former 'killing fields'. During Pol Pot's genocidal reign between 1975 and 1979, 1 million of Cambodia's 7 million people were murdered. Sophal was one of the few Christian survivors. This reign of repression for the church lasted for fifteen years. Even with the establishment of the pro-Vietnamese government in 1979 and the demise of the Khmer Rouge, the church was not recognised until 1990.

In August 1994, he and Deborah came to the Toronto Airport Fellowship and divine electricity coursed through them as they soaked in prayer. Sophal testified that the electricity that flowed through his body while on the carpet reminded him of what he received at the hand of the Khmer Rouge—except now it was absolute love that flowed through him.

On Sophal's return to Phnom Penh, the 'blessing' followed him. On the Sunday morning of 31 August, Sophal was sharing about what was happening in Toronto. People fell on the floor before he could finish the sermon. At the evening service the same thing happened.

Then it began to rain! People from the city began bringing all of the idols into the newly constructed Buddhist temple on the mountain outside Phnom Penh. Everyone knew that it was built for the Khmer Rouge and their artefacts. Suddenly, inhabitants saw a ball of fire coming from the sky and hitting the side of the building, causing the temple to move fifty metres—it was completely destroyed. A television crew was dispatched to the scene from the Phnom Penh station and interviewed the residents. Five Buddhist monks testified about the 'fire-ball.' One monk said that he was clinging to his bed for the entire fifty metres, but he was not injured. The monk felt happy and was rejoicing.

God destroyed the idols, but the people were left unharmed. Sounds like God's grace! That same day people witnessed two other Buddhist temples that were hit by 'fire-balls from heaven'. A new openness among the people to consider seriously the message of the Christian gospel was reported in the city in the aftermath. Isaiah 42:13 does say that 'the Lord will march out like a mighty man, like a warrior he will stir up his zeal; with a shout he will raise the battle cry and will triumph over his enemies'. During days of spiritual renewal in the Scriptures we see God's 'fire' falling: sometimes to consecrate the altars of our obedience like Elijah's experience in 1 Kings 18 as we confront the gods of this world; other times as a sign of his displeasure and judgement. Nadab and Abihu offered false fire in the temple and God acted out of his holiness and his 'fire' consumed them (Leviticus 10:1–3). God's fire causes the nations to tremble.

God's trumpet

Another interesting prophetic sign has been the blowing of the shophar. This was the national trumpet of the Israelites and it is still used today in Jewish synagogues. It was employed on military and religious occasions to summon the people—either to worship or to war. It was used to announce the presence of the Lord (2 Samuel 6:15; 1 Chronicles 15:28; Zechariah 9:14).[19] It would also announce the anointing of a king, as in 1 King 1:39, and the destruction of Jericho's walls, as in Joshua 6:1–20.

Interestingly, the Hebrew word for 'Jubilee', as in the Year of Jubilee, has the same root word as 'shophar'. It was a day to sound the trumpet of God and his deliverance from bondage, debts and slavery. At the Day of Atonement of the forty-ninth year, the sounding of a 'shophar' marked the onset of the jubilee year, a year of freedom. However, religious bondage and stony walls still exist in many hearts, homes, churches, cities and nations. We need God's trumpet blast as never before.

Sunday morning worship at the Toronto Airport Fellowship on 16 July, 1995 was interesting to say the least. Scott Holtz, an evangelist from Brooklyn, New York, preached the word and then blew the shophar. People began weeping, wailing, shaking and interceding with a passion. That morning the sound of God's trumpet was a call to prayer.

The anointing of God to blow the shophar came upon Scott after an encounter with the Lord in a renewal meeting in 1994. Since then he has been sounding the alarm in many of the cities of North America. Born and raised in a Jewish home, Scott came to embrace Yeshua (Jesus) as the Messiah as a young man. He has been an effective evangelist but even more so as the ability came upon him to wield this Old Testament weapon of war. An amazing series of events began to take place in his life where the blowing of the shophar had visual results. The following is a brief sketch of a few prophetic events that have been confirmed by witnesses when he was led to blow the trumpet of God.

In June 1994, after a time of waiting upon God, Scott was instructed by the Lord to go to Wall Street Stock Exchange and blow the ram's horn. Right there, in front of those venerable buildings along with his wife Dalit and a few believers, Scott blew his horn. The eerie sound rose up among the skyscrapers. God simply directed him to declare a 'sign' of God's impending action at this Mecca of the financial world. The next day the New York stock market shot up. It went on a spiral upward move for many months, breaking all the established records. Call it coincidence or the hand of God, but the signs don't stop here.

That same month Scott was preaching in St John's, the capital city of Newfoundland, Canada. Several of the pastors in the city made the unusual request that he blow the shophar on Signal Hill, overlooking the city and the Atlantic Ocean. It was here that Marconi transmitted the first wireless message from North America to Europe. When an army sets up to fight on any field of battle, they make sure they take the 'high ground'. There is such a place in the city of St John's, called Signal Hill. It was a miserable morning, which in spite of summer close at hand, is usual for that maritime city. The weather report was dismal with fog and drizzle in the forecast. But something dramatic was about to take place. As Scott blew the shophar and the believers gathered to pray for a spiritual breakthrough in the city, the dense fog began to split in two right over the harbour. They were amazed! One of the pastors actually saw one of the icebergs in the harbour break apart. They even have pictures displaying this interesting turn of events. It was taken as a 'sign' by this group of spiritual leaders in the city that God had heard their prayers. Even the local weather reporter was baffled that day on the radio. Only in the city of St John's was that intense cloud cover rolled back. Reports came out that the jet stream (high altitude winds that dictate weather patterns) had suddenly dipped over the city and only St John's received sunlight that day in the province. Interesting!

God has many ways of speaking to and through his

people. Sometimes he speaks without words just as Scott had witnessed the effect of God's trumpet in the face of earthly structures. Sometimes he speaks by heaven-sent fire or through physical acts (like babies falling on us). Prophetic signs come in many different ways. Again, each 'sign' must not be misinterpreted. Don't be like the children's story character Chicken Licken who ran around prophesying, 'The sky is falling, the sky is falling,' just because something fell on his head. Take time before God. Evaluate what has just happened around you. Does it have precedence in Scripture? Does it resonate with the character of God? If the answer is yes, then don't limit God by some formerly held perception. There are many Jericho walls that need to fall in the world and we need the validation of the Holy Spirit to direct us in his battle.

Indeed, we need to press into God's vast ocean of prophetic creativity. This goes beyond sight and sounds. He will use every part of the universe to declare his passion for mankind. He will use even the arts to capture us, his chief creation, as we will see in the next chapter.

8

PROPHETIC CREATIVITY

Sunday mornings at EastGate Christian Fellowship in Hamilton, Ontario are always very enlightening. This congregation is a satellite church of the Toronto Airport Christian Fellowship. My wife, Dianne, and I have been the planting pastors since the early days of 1996. During worship, flags will fly overhead and a prophetic dance may spontaneously accompany a song of praise. This is not some attention-grabbing ploy. These are believers who are genuinely being moved by the Spirit of God to act out our words of love of Jesus and the Father. It could be Judy, Laura or Shirley flowing in syncopation with the lyrics, underlining the truth of God's greatness.

At times I have been in tears as this prophetic creativity is being expressed during worship. Truths that I have found hard to tell God, like kneeling before him, laying my talents before him and other classic Christian concepts seem to come alive inside me. The Spirit of Jesus is not only the Spirit of prophecy, but also the Spirit of creativity.

He who brooded over the face of that unformed mass

in Genesis 1:2 and brought forth life as God spoke the command is again brooding over God's people. He is engendering divine creativity. He is reclaiming the arts today in all their wonder and potential. The Hebrew verb used here for the English word 'brooding' is *rachaph*. It is applied in Scripture, for example in Deuteronomy 32:11, to the resting of a bird over its young, to warm them and shield them.[20] This same word also appears in Jeremiah 33:9, where the response of the righteous to God was 'shaking' or 'trembling'.

I wonder if there is any connection with the shaking we have witnessed in the renewal meetings as the Holy Spirit descends? Could it be that he is releasing prophetic creativity as he did at creation?

In the Bible we see the creative mandate of the Holy Spirit, God's breath or *ruach* in Hebrew. Psalm 33:6 says that 'by the word of the Lord were the heavens made, their starry host by the breath (*ruach*/Spirit) of his mouth'. Psalms 104:30 praises the creator with these words: 'When you send your Spirit (*ruach*/breath), they are created, and you renew the face of the earth.' As God's Spirit has been hovering, blowing, brooding over believers around the world, bursts of prophetic creativity have followed in his wake. I'm not talking about a natural inclination to dance, draw, paint or write poetry. This creativity comes with the signature of God and it carries a message about the almighty.

God knows full well that the arts need to be reclaimed. There has been a disturbing, dehumanising trend in the art world. The artist, Robert Mapplethorpe, recently caused an uproar in America with a tax-funded exhibition of photographs depicting homosexual erotica.[21] There must be more to life than this!

Francis Schaeffer, the distinguished twentieth-century

philosopher, effectively demonstrated in his book *How Shall We Then Live?* that the decline of modern art into a state of fragmentation and despair is a manifestation of the prevailing world-view of despair. Men and women speak and sing and paint out of what fills the heart. Is it any wonder that the Holy Spirit should come upon us with a fresh infusion of hope and creativity to let the arts speak once more? The Spirit of the living God is pouring out new hope for the world.[22]

Prophetic art

Art that is God breathed can have a voice much like the prophetic word uttered in church. The imagery of creation is a voice for God. 'The heavens declare the glory of God; the skies proclaim the work of his hands,' so extols David the shepherd king in Psalm 19:1. A picture is worth a thousand words, even in God's economy. Stars, sky, the whole universe for that matter make proclamations about God. Old Testament prophets used imagery to communicate God's heart and now the Spirit is speaking volumes through prophetic paintings.

This has not been easy for me to embrace. I grew up in an evangelical church where the sanctuary walls were sterile—not even a stained-glass window could be found to distract a young mind during a lengthy sermon. The best art we had was a hand-painted banner that adorned the choir loft at the front of the church. Its terse statement, 'Be silent before the Lord' (Zechariah 2:13), always haunted me from above. The only way I could find any distraction was by counting the ceiling tiles or the number of hand gesticulations the preacher used. If only inspirational paintings had encircled the pews, I might have had an easier time on Sundays!

Many churches have a low view of representational art. It's probably a residue from the Reformation with its selective destruction of any Roman Catholic images that could have been falsely worshipped. They 'tidied up' with a vengeance and the places of worship became sterile. Now many evangelical churches are just beginning to rediscover the sacredness of the arts that emanate from the heart of our creator God. Prophetic art is coming back to the house of God.

On 15 June, 1995, the Reverend Rik Berry, pastor of Glen Erin Baptist Church, was our guest preacher at the Toronto Airport Christian Fellowship. His whole sermon revolved around two of his prophetic paintings and the biblical mandate for the coming 'harvest'. I had met Rik during seminary days and now our paths crossed again. During the previous winter I had the opportunity of ministering to Rik in the whole area of the arts. Rik is a gifted artist and I felt God encouraging me to speak prophetically into his life regarding a new release for Spirit-breathed painting. In short, prophetic painting—one that reveals more of God to humanity. Soon I was ministering to Rik who was now situated on the floor. I did not know, but at the time his first painting was already finished. The subject for that painting came in the form of a vision of 'The Lion of Judah' found in Revelation 5:1–5. The vision became concrete in the form of canvas and acrylic paint.

We had the privilege of a special viewing at the Ontario Renewal Network, a weekly pastoral gathering focused on sharing, intercession and renewal. Many people were visibly shaken by the impact of this enormous Lion roaring over the city of Toronto, and gifts of interpretation from the Spirit began expressing God's message about the authority of his Son. One person called out, 'There is the form of a wine glass in the poured-out position in the Lion's mouth'. Indeed, the Lord is pouring out his end-times anointing over the city.

The painting spoke more to us than Rik could have ever imagined. You see, the artist was not Rik Berry, but the almighty whose voice has been unleashed on the earth through his people. Rik describes this pictorial prophecy in his own words: 'When I first painted it I thought essentially of the city of Toronto. However, the CN Tower is at the foot of the picture. It represents telecommunications. I didn't consciously intend it, but one man suggested that it represents global communications—a revival in the airwaves with global results that will encompass the world.'

A second painting, called 'The Harvest', was displayed to the church that evening. The genesis for this work came in a completely different fashion. 'While John Wimber spoke at the Airport Fellowship in June 1994,' Rik explains, 'I found myself doing something foolish, almost militant . . . swaying with my hands open as if I was holding a scythe. I lived it out . . . dramatising it. Only later was I able to get the Spirit to interpret the action as that of a harvester going out into the fields already prepared.' We have already discussed the validity of prophetic mime, here it became the basis for God to speak a powerful prophetic image. Again, Rik interprets the painting.

'Notice that there are many people, harvesters, in the distance. There are other churches from my community all at work in the common field. The wheat is ready . . . and the harvesters reap what's ready. But the most powerful agent is not you or me—we don't have to come up with a neat evangelistic plan alone. It's the Holy Spirit. He is light.' (The image of a dove is in the light above the harvester.)

Rik is only one of a whole wave of artists freshly anointed to prophecy. It's not some new passing fad. Not only is artistic talent from God, but so is the unction to let it speak to our culture. Have you ever considered the life of Bezalel in Exodus 35–39? He was the chief artisan who decorated the Tabernacle. Did you know that Bezalel was the first person noted in the Bible as being filled with the Holy Spirit? Gene Edwards clarifies this connection in his book *State of the Arts*.

The Holy Spirit came upon someone who thereby became a prophet (Judges 6:34, Judges 11:29, Judges 13:25, 1 Samuel 10:5–6). In other words, the Holy Spirit enabled the prophet to proclaim the word of God. The Spirit of God here empowers Bezalel 'to devise artistic designs'. The implication is that the works of Bezalel will express, in the medium and in the language of art, the word of God.[23]

Prophetic song

As in the days of Bezalel, the word of God is again being broadcast through art, not just paint and paper art, but also through the beauty of 'prophetic song'. Let's define our terms. 'Singing in the Spirit' is not to be misunderstood as 'prophetic song'. As a newly baptised charismatic, I was enthralled by the absolute sense of worship and the presence of God as the church would spontaneously begin 'singing in the Spirit'. At times I actually looked around the room trying to identify the hidden conductor of such sweet melodies. There was none except the Spirit of God.

Paul urges the Ephesian believers, 'Do not get drunk on wine, which leads to debauchery. Instead, be filled with the Spirit. Speak to one another with psalms, hymns and spiritual songs' (Ephesians 5:18–19). This last phrase 'spiritual songs' is based on the Greek word *pneumatikas*. It is used in a similar context in 1 Corinthians 14: 26 as a 'revelation'.

In Pauline theology, these were songs 'such as the Holy Spirit inspired and gave utterance'. The emphasis is on charismatic worship. Paul alludes to this in his own personal testimony in 1 Corinthians 14:15—'I will sing with my spirit', meaning singing in tongues. Fresh oil has poured out on many congregations with this renewal and there has been wonderful worship and 'singing in the Spirit'.

There has been a fresh release of 'prophetic song'. 'Singing in the Spirit' is the believer's voice focused on God, but the 'prophetic song' is God's voice addressing his children. The means are the same, yet the focus is different.

God has been publicly singing to his children all around the world. It's a fulfilment, I believe, of Zephaniah 3:17—'He will rejoice over you with singing.' As the 'Spirit of prophecy' comes upon a congregation and worship band, there is often an unction to prophesy in song.

During the 'Times of Refreshing' conference in Sunderland, England, June 1995, God began to sing loud and clear. On the Saturday afternoon, one seminar was offered on worship and all worship leaders present were invited to join together for teaching and ministry. The room was jammed with 120 leaders from across England. Gary Sheldon, the conference worship leader from the St Louis Vineyard, spoke on the call to lead worship and I assisted with the ministry session that followed. A good time was had by all, as the church bulletin would say. I asked the Holy Spirit to come and release 'prophetic song' and then, from all over the room, these gifted singers and musicians began singing the word of the Lord. 'I am coming like fresh rain falling on this land,' went one song. They could have stood there for hours and sung God's heart as the Spirit intertwined melodies with words. Several came up to me and said, 'I have never done that before, singing the Lord's word to his people.' I'm sure that will not be the last time either, as the comforter comes afresh on these worship leaders during their own Sunday services.

Instead of fire bombs dropping on the city of Berlin, the fire of Holy Spirit was falling on that city in September 1995. At the union renewal meetings held at Christliches Zentrum Church, the church building that was built by Kaiser Wilhelm for his army officers, prophetic song came upon the worship team as new soldiers of the cross.

Some of the musicians were from the former East Berlin Orchestra and they were indeed set free to worship God. As the violin would carry on after a verse, you could hear the invocation of God's voice conferring his love upon us. Waves of power washed over me as I sat in the front pew, listening to the sweet sound of heaven coming through the violin. I wasn't the only one touched. You could see that many people in that crowd of approximately 1,000 were visibly affected by the prophetic song. I spoke with several of the leaders in the service to verify the fact that it wasn't just the effect of good music that was touching my emotions. Many that I interviewed had also received the same prophetic word of God's unconditional love as the violin played out the heavenly melody. It didn't stop there! The cello took up the theme with the piano and guitar following on in successive refrains. Minutes, hours, life-times could have passed by as the voice of the Lord came forth.

These Berlin musicians are now gathering together with other international psalmists to minister and prophesy in song. Words at times are not needed. A gift of interpretation is distributed liberally by the Spirit over the church and the intent of God's heart is understood.

This is not new and is not a singular manifestation of the present renewal. Throughout the Old Testament God's word came in the form of prophetic song and music. We have already discussed the prophetic worship offered up by the harpist in 2 Kings 3:15 that assisted Elisha to speak the word of the Lord before Jehoshaphat. David Blomgren speaks of those prophetic times in his book *The Song of the Lord*, with the following description:

> The schools of the prophets were instructed not only in the Law and the Scriptures but also in singing, especially psalm-singing. Eusebius, known as the father of church history, stated that the instruction in the school of the prophets was done by riddles, proverbs and chanting of sacred and secular poems and by singing songs.

Sendry, a Jewish scholar, says that it is undeniable that the 'sons of the prophets' received systematic and thorough instruction in music.[24]

All the effort in maturing the prophetic gift through song and instruments was not in vain. A brief look at the Old Testament witnesses to the sheer amount of God's word that came to us through song. In LaMar Boschman's book, *The Prophetic Song*, there is an eight-page list of scriptures that were sung by prophets of old.[25] He states, 'The Psalms do not have a monopoly on the "songs of the Spirit", for all ten major Bible divisions contain examples. The prophetic song is as fresh as today's move of the Spirit, and yet as old as the word itself.'[26]

We will never forget the first 'Catch the Fire' conference held at the Toronto Airport Christian Fellowship in October 1994, as wave after wave of prophetic song filled the auditorium. Believers from every continent had gathered together to seek the Lord, yet the Lord was seeking them. He loves to sing over his children. Joanne McFadder, a gifted prophetic singer from Kansas City Vineyard, declared God's heart to his people. My immediate response was, Oh how he loves us! The terms of endearment that were sung by the Lord through Joanne were shocking at times: 'Let me hold you in my arms . . . Let me embrace you.'

After the Levitical psalmists, like the family of Asaph, with the musicians and trumpeters and singers joined in unison as with one voice . . . then the temple of the Lord was filled with a cloud, and the priests could not perform their service' (2 Chronicles 5:13–15). It probably means that they couldn't stand up!

There is a day coming when music will so fill the Church that we too will be on our faces as the cloud of God's glory descends. I believe there is also new music coming from a Spirit-anointed Church to the world. We will receive the beat of heaven and a generation of people presently lost to the kingdom will come to hear the sounds. The Holy Spirit is reviving the arts today in all their fullness and they will, through the vehicle of a renewed Church, fulfil the purposes of God.

9

THE BIBLICAL RELEASE OF PROPHECY

There I was, an eager twenty-year-old charismatic Bible school student stuck in the middle of a non-charismatic youth prayer meeting. After some Scripture was discussed, the real fun came when the twenty or more teens began to pray. It was one of those around-the-circle prayers that started with the leader. I wasn't a rocket scientist, but I figured out quite quickly that I was about number eighteen to pray before the fearless leader was to give the concluding 'amen'. She was actually a respected high school teacher in the city and came from a very traditional church. I had to be on my best Baptist behaviour.

But something went wrong, or maybe right, with the prayers. One student after another began to call out to God to speak to them. The pleading and petitions increased as the prayers went around the circle. 'Come, Spirit of the living God. Come right here and now and speak to us, your people!' Each one seemed to be seeking to outdo the next person in how they could plead with God to actually speak to them. I was in a jam! Being a secret charismatic, I didn't know what to do. With every prayer a prophetic urge increased inside me. All I could do was to hold it in. Then came my turn.

'Shada mi cratsa . . .' exploded from my lips as I began to give a message in tongues, followed by an interpretation. Was I ever glad to get it over with! However, dead silence fell over the room. The next two prayer warriors were hardly audible. I guess I ruined their meeting. Worst of all, the respected leader curtly closed the prayer time and went on to bless an assortment of sweet breads that we were about to receive. It could well have been sawdust instead of cakes that covered the kitchen table. I felt the scorn of all those present.

They didn't want their prayers answered. They didn't want to hear God speak to them. They just wanted to plead with him, asking him to come in a hundred different ways. This young Bible college student got a most valuable lesson during that summer of service—both he and the Church needed to be taught on the subject of prophecy.

Some of that teaching is actually hidden in the meaning of the five different Hebrew and Aramaic root words translated in our English text as 'prophecy'. They have a wealth of meaning and actually describe the way in which God's inspiration comes. Two of the words, *ro'eh* and *chozeh*, underline the passive experience of receiving the prophetic message from God, while the other three words, *massa*, *naba* and *nataf* describe the active experience of communicating God's message to the audience.[27]

Ro'eh

The word *ro'eh* literally means 'a seer' and it occurs twelve times in the Hebrew text of the Old Testatment. Essentially, the root *ra'ah* means 'to look at' or 'behold'. This word is used of the prophet in his 'seeing' or perceiving of God's message, especially, although not exclusively, with reference to the visionary. This word describes distinctively the prophetic revelation of the prophet through visions.[28]

Chozeh

Here is another word translated in our English Bibles as 'prophet'. It also carries the base meaning of 'a seer'. This word is used sixteen times in the Hebrew text. David Blomgren makes the distinction between these two words, stating that 'although these two terms, *ro'eh* and *chozeh* may be used interchangeably, CHOZEH seems to be the broader term used to refer to either cognitive or visionary perception'.[29]

Massa

The Hebrew term *massa* and its root *nasah* are used a total of seventy times in the Old Testament to identify prophecy. It actually means 'a burden' and it reveals the response of the one receiving God's message—it comes like a weight or burden upon them. That is what happened to me in the prayer meeting I described above. A literal weight came upon my body. Read through Isaiah 13–23 and time after time 'the burden of the Lord' comes upon Isaiah as he speaks God's word of rebuke and judgement over Babylon, Moab, Damascus, Egypt, Dumah, Arabia and Tyre.

Both Zechariah and Malachai use the phrase 'the burden of the word of the Lord' in King James English Bible, while the NIV uses the word 'oracle' to describe a strong prophetic message from God. It's interesting to note the blending of prophetic terms in the opening salvo of Habakkuk's book of prophecy: 'The burden which Habakkuk . . . did see' (Habakkuk 1:1, KJV).

David Blomgren goes on to add another interesting gloss to the word *massa*.

> This same Hebrew word, however, is also descriptive of the lifting up of the soul in the prophetic flow of the temple musicians as exemplified in the master musician Chenaniah who was master of 'song', (Hebrew *massa* here is a 'joy or literally a lifting up', Ezekiel 24:25). Also implicit within this word is the concept that the purpose behind the prophetic word, even when judgemental, is restorative. Even when denunciation is in order because of sin, it is a 'lifting up' prophecy, intended to bring them higher in God's ways. Indeed, the main concept behind this word *massa* is that of a lifting up, not a weighing down.[30]

Naba

This graphic word for prophecy occurs no less than 435 times in the Old Testament. The Aramaic and Hebrew word *naba* basically means 'to bubble up, to gush forth, to pour forth'.[31] It gives a clear image of the activity of the Spirit of God flowing from our innermost being as a river of life. This time, however, the river is a river of words—words from God. Amos 3:8 says, 'The Sovereign Lord has spoken—who can but [*naba*] prophesy?. Joel 2:28 says, 'Your sons and daughters will [*naba*] prophesy.' That's what happened to me in that youth prayer meeting. There was a 'bubbling up' within me to communicate God's heart. Some theologians actually consider this term to describe an ecstatic aspect of prophecy.[32]

Nataf

Here is the second Hebrew word for prophecy that describes a dynamic form of communication. The prophetic message is in essence an interplay between a reception of God's words and the giving of those words through a human vessel, like you or me. While *naba* described the communicating of a prophecy like words that bubbled up from within, *nataf* pictures a flow of words that actually drop upon the messenger 'as drops of rain'.[33] This Hebrew word is used in the Scriptures a total of twenty-one times. In Micah 2:6–11 it is used four times as a descriptive term for prophecy. 'It is not only a flow as water from the prophet's lips, gushing forth as a fountain, but it is also to be viewed as rain drops, falling from heaven . . . the prophetic word is a word dropped by God from heaven as rain.'[34]

I have often experienced this rain of God's thoughts upon me as I preach or pray over people. They come one by one and at times I feel embarrassed as I wait for more insights to fall upon me. It is normal. One of the meanings of the word 'to prophesy' is just that—waiting for rain from heaven.

However tedious the process, 'prophecy is an indication of God's approval and blessing on the congregation because it shows that God is actively present in the assembled church'—so affirms Wayne Grudem in his book *The Gift of Prophecy*[35]. More prophecy, Lord! Send your inspiration into your Church because it's a sign that you are present in the midst of us.

When one reviews Paul's teaching on the prophetic gift in the epistles, this conclusion is well supported. The apostle's directive to the Corinthian congregation, 'You can all prophesy in turn' (1 Corinthians 14:31) echoes

Joel 2:28's promised river of revelation falling upon the young and old, sons and daughters. In this river even the poor will prophesy by the Spirit. It is true that some commentators would interpret the 'all' as limited to just the order of the prophets. However, Paul called all the saints to 'eagerly desire spiritual gifts, especially the gift of prophecy' (1 Corinthians 14:1), suggesting that this manifestation was open to the whole believing community.[36]

Let's consider for a moment Paul's basic theme. The Corinthian church probably questioned Paul regarding the comparative value of tongues and prophecy in their services. The apostle was responding to their over-emphasis on tongue speaking. He never devalues the gift as he boldly testifies to these zealous tongue speakers: 'I thank God that I speak in tongues more than all of you' (1 Corinthians 14:18). He was talking of his own private devotional life. In his view of appropriate worship in a local New Testament church, prophecy was *the* desired demonstration of the Spirit's presence. Why? Because this manifestation of the Spirit focused on others. It focused on edifying the body of Christ with messages of strength, encouragement and comfort (1 Corinthians 14:3). You can hardly go wrong if you want to bring life and courage to the saints. That was the function of the gifts of the Spirit in the first place: 'to each one the manifestation of the Spirit is given for the common good' (1 Corinthians 12:7).

Nor was prophecy intended to put fear into God's people. I'll never forget my first trip to Japan and the wall of fear that I had to dismantle. Somehow the meetings were publicised with the announcement that a prophet from Canada would be ministering. I've never used that title. In fact, I'm wary when people brashly tell me that they are prophets. Red lights of pride, position grabbing and influence pedalling go off in my head. However, as I taught and then gave words of knowledge during ministry time, a strange thing happened. It was as if the believers were hanging their heads, not wanting to establish eye contact with me. You could almost hear their hearts talking: 'If he sees me he will ask me to stand and prophesy over me.'

I later found out that so-called prophets had been through the churches in the area with devastating results. They would get people to stand up and commence a description of their sins, shortcomings and failures. Like Old Testament prophets without New Testament grace, they sullied the whole prophetic gift to these dear people. I did not embarrass them. Rather, I openly shared my own failures in the receiving and giving of prophecies. By the second day, the air had cleared. The fear was gone and many were blessed.

There is a radical difference between Old and New Testament prophecy. *Scripture* was penned by these old covenant saints. In no way would modern-day prophetic insights be considered to be equal to Scripture. Gordon Fee, in his excellent book *God's Empowering Presence*, suggests a proper theme for present-day prophecies: 'The nature of the prophecy was also understood to be of a different kind, precisely because of their present eschatological existence. A prophet who speaks encouragement to the church in its 'between times' existence speaks a different kind of word from the predominant word of judgement on ancient Israel.'[37]

There was also a different function for prophecy in the new convenant community. Gordon Fee goes on to give the following insightful summary:

The actual function of prophecy in the Pauline churches is more difficult to pin down. If our view of Galatians 2:2, 1 Timothy 1:18, (cf 4:14) and 1 Timothy 4:14 is correct, then, on the one hand, the Spirit directs the lives of his servants in specific ways—sometimes they are singled out for the ministry the Spirit empowers (1 Timothy 1:18, 1 Timothry 4:14) and sometimes they are directed to undertake a difficult mission to Jerusalem (Galatians 2:2). On the other hand, the Spirit also reminds the Church, probably repeatedly, that the words of Jesus concerning the increase of evil in the end (1 Timothy 4:1) are being confirmed. It was probably a misguided but heeded prophetic utterance that the Day of the Lord had already come (2 Thessalonions 2:2) that led to the dicers in Thessalonica. In 1 Corinthians, 14, yet another picture emerges of how the community regularly experiences the prophetic spirit. In the case of believers the Spirit speaks encouragement and edification, and in the case of unbelievers he lays bare their hearts in such a way as to lead to repentance. All of this suggests that 'prophecy' was a widely experienced phenomenon, which had as its goal the building up of the people of God so as to come to maturity in Christ (Ephesians 4:11–16).[38]

Releasing prophecy in your life and church requires several important decisions. There seem to be six major affirmations that I need to make continually as I minister to people. If any one of these elements is lacking in my heart, then the prophecy comes out flat or misses the mark altogether.

The Spirit's fire

'Do not put out the Spirit's fire—do not treat prophecies with contempt,' Paul exhorts the congregation in Thessalonica (1 Thessalonians 5:19). A harsh attitude against prophecy is tantamount to grieving the Spirit. What else could the Holy Spirit feel when a Christian community refuses to let his fire light upon them? It's like dowsing a barbecue with cold water just as the family is about to eat. It's like pouring buckets of water on a winter's fire that brings warmth to all.

Sounds incredible, doesn't it? Yet that goes on weekly in our hearts and churches. 'Do not grieve the Holy Spirit,' Paul cautions regarding a believer's relationship with the Holy Spirit (Ephesians 4:30). The spirit is a real person with feelings, thoughts and wishes. He wants to speak and we need to welcome his presence. It is the fire of the Holy Spirit that will bring his voice.

An eager desire

Paul makes it clear in his teaching on the gifts of the Spirit in 1 Corinthians that we are to be zealous when it comes to giving prophetic words in the assembly. In several connected passages we see God's opinion of prophecy in the life of his children. The short list goes like this: 'But eagerly desire the greater gifts'; 'and eagerly desire spiritual gifts, especially the gift of prophecy'; 'try to excel in gifts that build up the church'; 'therefore, my brothers, be eager to prophesy' (1 Corinthians 12:31; 14:1, 12, 39).

The Greek word Paul used for 'desire' is *zeloo*, from which we derive the English word 'zeal'. We are to become modern-day zealots for this ministry of building up the body of Christ with prophetic words. Time and again I've received deep-seated comfort and encouragement when the word of the Lord is brought forth in church or during personal prayer ministry. When praying for others I often seek God for a 'word' that will come alongside and help.

By faith

The way we got in is the way we go on! We came into the Christian life and the fullness of the Spirit by faith and we should not expect any change of plans. In Romans 12: 6, the apostle Paul teaches that 'we have different gifts, according to the grace given us. If a man's gift is prophesying, let him use it in proportion to his faith.' A buried talent does not please the master. The 'I was afraid' excuse will not work. Just tell the congregation or person to whom you are called to speak— 'I believe the Lord would say . . .'. That gives both you and the one receiving the word a way to reflect on its message without your pretending to be infallible. Only the word in Scripture is infallible.

Often when the Spirit directs me to give a prophecy in a church or call out certain individuals, I have nothing but a sense of compassion and one or two words. Over the years, as I have stepped out, God has proven to be faithful and gives many revelations that flow out of his heart. It's just like pulling tissues out of the Kleenex box. They come out one at a time. Provision comes for those who give what they have.

Fan into flame

We, like Timothy, need to hear these words from Paul, his dear mentor: 'I remind you to fan into flame the gift of God, which is in you through the laying on of my hands'; 'Do not neglect your gift, which was given you through a prophetic message when the body of elders laid their hands on you' (2 Timothy 1:6:1 Timothy 4:14). Gifts of the Spirit wane and fade with lack of use. With the gathered elders, Paul prophesied certain callings and giftings concerning young Timothy's life. Possibly the messages were to do with a significant role he was to have in the Church. But now the prophesied word and the accompanying spiritual gift were like dormant coals of fire just waiting to be stirred up into flame. Let the passion for ministering the Father's voice of love to the world be your goal. Get soaked in the Holy Spirit!

Flow of love

The opening salvo of 1 Corinthians 14, the central chapter on the prophetic gift, is not a word about the value or practice of prophecy but the motivation for prophecy: 'Follow the way of love.' Any spiritual gift ministered through and to God's people that does not have love as its foundation will tear down and not build up. Paul's 'love chapter', 1 Corinthians 13, is strategically placed between the listing of spiritual gifts in chapter 12 and the practice of the same in chapter 14. Love is the only basis for the prophetic.

As a young charismatic I sought to have my spiritual gun notched with all the nine gifts of the Spirit, manifesting each one at least once. I was becoming pride-filled and obnoxious. It took a few of God's wise counsellors to keep me from playing with the power. Let love for broken sheep be your goal no matter what you discern as the root sin. We don't need to enact God's wrath. The one who 'never broke a bruised reed' will show you how to flow in love as you prophesy.

Test the word

No prophetic word you give or are given ever has official status. Jesus said, 'Heaven and earth will pass aways, but my words will never pass away' (Matthew 24:35). His word is the only word with an independent, unscrutinised authority. With the same breath that Paul uses to call the Thessalonians back to the practice of prophecy, he issues the command to 'test everything; hold on to the good; avoid every kind of evil' (1 Thessalonians 5:20–21).

Again Dr Fee has wisdom on this subject.

> The combined evidence of 1 Thessalonians 5:21–22 and 1 Corinthians 12:10 and 14:29 indicates that all prophesying must be 'discerned' by the Spirit-filled community. That is almost certainly the first intent of the gift of the 'discernment of Spirits' in 1 Corinthians 12:10, since the cognate verb of the noun 'discernment' appears in 14:29 as the needed response to prophetic utterances, just as interpretation is needed with tongues.[39]

We are called to test together each word that is brought forth in the assembly by the Church, God's Spirit-filled community. This whole subject is discussed in the appendix 'What to Do When You Receive a Prophetic Word.' This will help as you get through the testing stage and as you begin applying God's prophetic words, visions and signs to your life.

In the meantime, take courage from the experience of the Church. Strong words and manifestations accompanying a prophetic message have been a part of our Christian heritage. It's time to refresh our memory.

10

THE PROPHETIC IN REVIVAL HISTORY

Like a golden thread woven through the fabric of Church history, prophetic gifts have graced the body of Christ. This prophetic heritage of the Church is a reflection of the glory of God to our culture. From the earliest days of the Apostolic Fathers in the second century to the Reformation period and the Latter Rain Movement of 1948–51, revelation has been evident.

There is an identifiable link between the reviving presence of the Spirit and the voice of the Spirit. When the comforter comes he often brings words of comfort mediated through God's people. We are experiencing that same phenomenon at the Toronto Airport Fellowship and in the renewal meetings that are springing up world wide. An exhaustive study of the prophetic in Church history could in itself be the subject of a book. For the purpose of understanding the relationship of the prophetic and the Church, I would like to review some of the historical highlights.

Apostolic Fathers

Not only was the New Testament written against the backdrop of a massive revival, but the Apostolic Fathers (AD70-200) also wrote during seasons of refreshing from the Lord Irenaeus, Justin Martyr and Tertullian. All recount the continuing work of the gifts of the Spirit in the Church. Richard Riss, in his series *Tongues and Other Miraculous Gifts in the Second Through Nineteenth Centuries*, suggests a reasoned approach to their letters and documents.

In the early history of the Church the gift of tongues was closely associated with prophecy. When the second-century author Irenaeus quoted Acts 10: 46, he substituted the word 'prophecy' where the biblical passage specifies 'tongues'. 'These miraculous gifts in general tend to be closely associated with one another, and accounts of tongues and prophecy are often included in accounts of healings, miracles, revelation and visions.'[40]

Justin Martyr wrote to his friend Trypho about 'gifts of prophecy' in the plural in approximately AD 148: 'From the fact that even to this day the gifts of prophecy exist among us Christians . . . Now if you look around, you can see among us both men and women endowed with gifts from the Spirit of God.' This discourse with Trypho was in the context of an overall discussion of other charismatic gifts. Prophecy was flowing in those early days of the Church along with a host of powerful spiritual encounters.[41]

Montanists

In AD 206, Tertullian of Carthage, the father of Latin theology, became a member of the Montanists, a widespread prophetic movement that lasted into the fifth century. In his work *A Treatise on the Soul*, Tertullian describes that third-century renewal in this fashion:

> For seeing that we acknowledge spiritual charismata, or gifts, we too have merited the attainment of the prophetic gift, although coming after John the Baptist. We have now amongst us a sister whose lot it has been to be favoured with sundry gifts of revelation, which she experiences in the Spirit by ecstatic vision amidst the sacred rites of the Lord's day in the church: she converses with angels, and sometimes even with the Lord; she both sees and hears mysterious communications; some men's hearts she understands, and to them who are in need she distributes remedies.[42]

Dr Kenneth Latourette, in his foundational book *A History of Christianity*, defends this movement which was severely persecuted by the established Church. He summarises the impact of the Montanists in this way:

> It had itinerant preachers supported by the gifts of the faithful, and in time seems to have been fairly well organized, with the head living in Phrygia. It prized the records of the teachings of Christ and his apostles, but it believed, although not contradicting what had been said there, that the Holy Spirit continued to speak through prophets, and among these it included women. It stressed a high standard of Christian living among Christian communities into which laxity was beginning to creep.[43]

Persecution of the Montanists may have been based on several issues. They did teach an imminent return of the Lord. The concept of an early return of Christ was not new, nor was it exclusively a tenet of the Montanists, as we find several allusions to it in the epistles and Revelation.[44] However, they gave dates and places which we know is not scriptural. Another reason why they were ostracised was probably cultural. Eusebius, an opponent of this movement, criticised the prophetic style. He reported that Montanus, the founder of the movement, 'suddenly fell into frenzy and convulsions. He began to be ecstatic and to speak and to talk strangely, prophesying contrary to the custom which belongs to the tradition and succession of the church from the beginning.'[45] It's hard to put new wine into old wine skins. Even now the same issues arise as fresh oil and new wine fill the Church.

Gregory

During the dark night of the soul in the Church, when the word of the Spirit almost became non-existent, there were still some shining prophetic voices heard in the land. Gregory, the pupil of Origen, in the fourth century was blessed with prophetic gifts and miracles. By Christ's mighty name he even commanded rivers to change their course and caused a lake, which had provoked a dispute among some covetous brethren, to dry up. Moreover, his predictions of things to come equalled in quality those of the great prophets before him.[46]

Genevieve of Paris

Genevieve of Paris accurately prophesied God's intervention over the city and called the believers to fast and pray as Attila the Hun was preparing to invade Paris in AD 451. The seemingly invincible army suddenly changed the course of its march and Paris was saved.[47]

Martin Luther

The Reformation was more than just a return to the light and to the Scriptures. Martin Luther taught on the value of the prophetic in his commentary on Joel 2:28—'For what are all other gifts, however numerous they may be, in comparison with this gift, when the Spirit of God himself, the eternal God, descends into our hearts, yea, into our bodies, and dwells in us, governs, guides and leads us? Thus with respect to this declaration of the prophet, prophecy, visions and dreams are, in truth, one precious gift.'[48]

Martin Luther was not just an armchair theologian. After wrestling with God in prayer for his sick friend Philip Melanchthon, he operated under a prophetic gift and declared to him, 'Be of good cheer, Philip, you shall not die.' As a result, a gift of healing was released and his dying friend was revived.[49]

The 'French prophets'

On the back of the Reformation, an amazing story of the 'French prophets' emerged. They are also known as 'the little prophets of the Cevennes', named after the young age of those who prophesied and the Cevennes mountains where they hid from persecution.

There had been a form of religious freedom for the Protestants in France since 1598 and the Edict of Nantes. However, in 1685 Louis XIV revoked the treaty and persecution returned. Like the Montanist movement, the 'French prophets' experienced strong convulsions and ecstatic movements as the word of the Lord was being proclaimed. To a large extent this was the contentious issue with the French church and government.

Thousands were martyred, many fled to England, others became entrenched in the mountains. Those who attempted to defend themselves between 1701 and 1710 were called the 'Camisards'. Miracles, healings, tongues and prophecy flowed in their meetings. The anointing seemed to be very contagious. Within a year of the first prophetic word given by a young girl in February 1688, there were a thousand prophets.[50]

One peasant, called Halmede, had a twelve-year-old son who had received the blessing. It wasn't a blessing to him, knowing that many households were massacred with such news. The local parish priest counselled the father that a forced fast with added beatings would stop his son from prophesying. But to no avail. Halmede returned in a short while with the same complaint. The last hope offered was the use of a snake skin as a charm or amulet which would be placed over the boy's head when he began to shake and prophesy. However, when this was attempted the child was shaken with a violent trembling and with a loud voice he shouted out the displeasure of the Lord over the sinful act that the father was committing. Then, like a bolt of lightening, Halmede was struck and began to weep tears of repentance. Within a few days he also became a shaking prophet like his son with gifts of revelation and knowledge.[51]

The common manifestations of the 'French prophets' were as follows: falling to the ground, groaning from the chest, jerks, visions, prophesying in perfect French when 'patois' was their only spoken language and a host of other gifts of the Spirit and miracles. One man named Jean Cavalier testified that God's presence would often come upon him and he would experience 'the jerks' and at times fall to the ground. This lasted for nine months, until one Sunday morning prayer time in his house when

God loosed his tongue and he prophesied after an extended period of shaking. Children as young as fourteen months prophesied the word of the Lord in impeccable Parisian French. They often spoke of the angelic song that would be heard in their meetings. There were even signs in the sky as fire would fall from heaven to blind the eyes of their enemies.[52] These revelations were usually focused on winning the lost in their midst and encouraging the saved. Yet when they fled to London for refuge many were taunted. A puppet play was even written, mocking their experiences of God.[53]

In their defence, Mr A. Bost, the 1707 chronicler who recorded their testimonies while in their London exile, affirmed that 'just one of them was worth a thousand of us'.[54] In his final reflections he asks these stirring questions, 'We have seen the declarations in our Holy Bible which announce so clearly that God will not cease to manifest himself in his church through many signs of his power. Do we even desire these signs? Or at least do we explore their absence?[55]

The Swedish prophets

Shaking prophecies didn't stop there. *The Evangelical Gazette of Berlin*, in March 1846, published an account of an extraordinary revival taking place in Sweden. The revival began in 1844 in Smaland, the poorest province of the country. Simple villagers, not knowing how to read or write, experienced an outpouring of the Spirit and began prophesying in perfect Swedish. They were called the 'roestars', which literally means the yellers or proclaimers, like John 1:23—'The voice of one calling out in the desert.' They too would tremble and shake both before a word was given and during it. They would lie on the ground or remain standing for up to two hours while the revelation was proclaimed. It seemed that they were shut up with God and their senses were locked away in him. Even the persecutors who tried to stop them would at times be seized with the same prophetic manifestations and became 'roestars' themselves!

Cane Ridge exhorters

Of course, there are other kinds of prophetic manifestations in modern Church history. In the 1801 Cane Ridge Revival, there were groups of believers in their midst called 'spontaneous exhorters'. Literally hundreds became prophetic preachers during those days. Mark Gali, in his article in the periodical *Church History*, states: 'Literally hundreds of people became spontaneous exhorters, excitedly giving advice or tearful warnings. Almost anyone—women, small children, slaves, the shy, the illiterate, could exhort with great effect.[56]

This one event in American Church history was the spark that 'ignited the explosion of evangelical religion which soon reached into every corner of American life'.[57] The strong prophetic manifestations in their midst only spurred on revival fires in the United States.

The Belgian Congo prompters

Akin to the 'spontaneous exhorters' of Cane Ridge is what the WEC missionaries called 'the prompters'. During the 1953 revival in the Belgian Congo they came face to face with 'the prompters', inspired speakers in the congregation who would begin to preach prophetically to the unconverted and unrepentant. Those who were in great agony of soul would come through to peace with God as 'the prompters' would speak out 'Jesus is ready to forgive! Think back! There is still more to confess! The big sin still remains!'[58] We could do with a few more of those in the twentieth-century Church.

The Latter Rain

Almost during this same time in North America, there was a renewal called the Latter Rain movement. In February 1948, the Holy Spirit fell on the students of Sharon Orphanage and School, a small Bible school in North Battleford, Saskatchewan, Canada. The world soon heard of the outpouring that was marked by the manifestation of prophesy and the intensity of God's presence in worship. Like prairie fire, the restoration movement swept through congregations in both Canada and the United States. Within a year, Elim Bible Institute in Lima, New York became one of the renewal centres. Their annual spring convention in 1949 was sheer glory. Carlton Spencer, the President's son, went on to explain the marks of this divine visitation.

> Most gracious indeed were the gifts of the Spirit in operation in the meetings: some of them entirely new, others in a greater anointing and power and others operating in new ways. In most every service a spirit of worship prevailed. At times the congregation would break forth in heavenly chorus with prophetical solos interspersed . . . At times during the Convention there were ministries of laying of hands with prophecy confirming calls and gifts imparted by the Lord.[59]

Richard Riss has reflected on the overall effect of the movement in his book *Latter Rain*. He concludes his review of the data: 'The Latter Rain movement provided a tremendous impetus to the people in many Pentecostal circles to seek to exercise the gift of prophecy . . . an important influence upon at least some portions of the Charismatic movement almost thirty years later.'[60]

The close of the century has arrived and the Church is again finding the infectious joy and power of the Holy Spirit. He is again causing the gifts to operate in 'new ways'; even some operations of the gifts are 'entirely new' as was the case at the Elim Bible Institute. Serendipity has come and we are indeed 'surprised', if not 'surprised by joy'. All through the ages, the Church of the living God has encountered his almighty presence. He is reshaping us so that we all may become 'roestars', shouters of his grace. The precious Holy Spirit is even now forming God's prophetic army which will bring in the 'harvest'.

11

LET THE PROPHETIC ARMY ARISE!

Hyuang heard about me through a telephone call. I had been preaching in Seoul, Korea during the summer of 1996 and my translator, Paul, communicated to him a 'prophetic word' that I had received about his manufacturing company. Hyuang and Paul had been involved some years ago in starting this business together with another university friend from Seoul, and the 'word' got his attention. Some details I had known regarding an upcoming business transaction were uncanny to this savvy businessman—he wanted to meet me. God was getting Hyuang's attention.

It was my last meeting in the city and Hyuang kindly came to the service, waiting to meet me. There was an unusual prophetic anointing that night and I eventually prophesied over approximately two hundred people without stopping until the stroke of midnight. Throughout the marathon session, Hyuang was standing at the front of the church listening and watching. He saw men and women alike being overcome by the presence of God as I spoke very simple words to them about their families and jobs.

Now it was his turn. In the confines of my hotel room, Hyuang told me that he had never been in a meeting like that before and he too wanted to receive prayer. 'O Lord, I'm tired and I don't have an ounce of anointing left but help me now,' I whispered to the Lord. By faith I began to speak affirming words of God's love over Hyuang. Out of that flow of love came one sentence: 'Your father was an army sergeant.' His mouth dropped open and out came the words, 'Yes, you're right!' God really had his attention now. Over the next few minutes the heavy army clothes came off his heart as God's love poured in. Hyuang prayed with me to receive the Lord into his life that night. I believe that a prophetic demonstration was God's key.

What will it take to give this world a reason for living? We've tried many well-intentioned programmes to lure people to Christ. We've even tried to advertise them into the kingdom with slick media presentations. I'm convinced that only a bold prophetic people can help the dying to hear God's message of mercy.

An end-time prophetic army is beginning to join ranks all over the world. Freshly anointed saints are now flowing in the Holy Spirit—the river of life. The prophetic Church is forming on the land and Erma Bombeck's forlorn humanity who've 'lost their way' will soon hear and see the way to the Father.

You don't have to be some superstar evangelist—just available to the Holy Spirit. Jesus always asks his disciples to give out to the people that which we have in our hands (Mark 6:38). He wants to take the five loaves and two fishes of our life and feed the hungry. He wants us to be available to receive prophetic insights, visions and trances, even allowing our bodies to mime a message of hope. Stay in the presence of the Holy Spirit and it will be proved true in your life that your God is a speaking God.

Let the creative flow of the Spirit bring a life-giving message to your world through prophetic art or song. The enemy has corrupted these vehicles of communication for centuries. It's time for a 'renewed Church' to claim back the arts and in the process preach Christ with great effect.

It's time to throw caution to the wind. It's time to step out with a word of encouragement or healing for your neighbour or colleague. Maybe you will meet someone in your own local McDonalds or cafe. Maybe you will be surprised by their kind response and the open door of witness.

The prophetic gift must break out of the confines of our morning worship services. If you've received 'words' for a believer at church, you can also receive 'words' for unbelievers in the world. The process is the same. It may start with a picture, scripture verse or just an impression, but you have a message from God to them. It's not something to hide under your basket or keep in your boat. Peter the apostle was such a blessing to the Lord's work because he was the one who got out of the boat and walked on water. All Jesus needed to say to Peter was 'come' and he launched out into a whole new realm of trust. We have received an equal mandate. The world is watching and waiting. Let's begin to put prophecy into practice!

APPENDIX

WHAT TO DO WHEN YOU RECEIVE PROPHETIC WORDS

In the foyer of the Toronto Airport Christian Fellowship a borchure adorns the front shelf. It's entitled, 'What to Do When You Receive Prophetic Words.' This is not playing 'catch up' to the 'Toronto blessing'. The article was written by John Arnott and is clearly labelled and dated: Toronto Airport Christian Fellowship, 6 December 1993. Prophecy had been flowing in our church, and our senior pastor wanted to fine tune the prophetic in order to bring all the best from God's heart for his children. The prophetic must be pastored. It can either be one of the greatest blessings in a congregation, or one of the greatest curses. Wild-eyed prophets can drop emotional bombs all over the Church, or the gift can be a wonderful blessing when believers focus on restoration and love. This booklet has helped to make prophecy a blessing at the Airport Fellowship and in many other congregations. Indeed, copies have circled the globe—we have to restock the shelf almost daily.

Prophets and the gift of prophecy

In the New Testament there is both the gift of prophecy, that all may aspire to (1 Corinthians, 12) and the office of a prophet that carries with it many more strictures. Personal prophetic words are reliable when coming from recognised leaders in the Church who fulfil the office of a prophet and who have a track-record for accuracy and accountability. There are several examples in the New Testatment. Philip received a word for the Ethopian in Acts 8:30. Peter received a word for Cornelius in Acts 10:20. The prophet Agabus predicted a famine in Acts 11:28 which was a word for the whole Church. In Acts 23:10, Agabus warned Paul of his coming arrest. In Acts 27:22, Paul gives a prophetic warning about the shipwreck and the saving of lives.

A word of prophecy can be a source of tremendous blessing and encouragement, and an event that can be pivotal for your faith, to believe God for greater things. However there can be opportunities for misunderstandings and difficulties. For this reason, I want to discuss some factors and outline some Scripture guidelines, safeguards and cautions so that you get the greatest benefit from this wonderful ministry. The purpose of prophecy is not to cast a person into confusion of disillusionment, but to build them up with edification, exhortation and comfort according to 1 Corinthians 14:3.

Prophetic words in the Church

1 Corinthians 12:10 teaches that the Holy spirit gives different gifts as he determines. The gifts are different, just as the parts of our bodies are different. That is what makes up the body—the Church. We are taught eagerly to

desire the greater gifts (1 Corinthians 12:31). We are to excel in the gifts that build up the Church (1 Corinthians 14:12). Prophecy, when given to the whole Church, is to build up and encourage the believers (1 Corinthians 14:22). All of this must be done for the strengthening of the Church—God's people (1 Corinthians 14:26). Usually, two or three prophecies in a public meeting are enough, and they should be carefully weighed by the leadership (1 Corinthians 14:29). Verse 31 teaches that we can all prophesy in turn, so we can learn and be encouraged. There is a learning curve here; and also, the 'prophets' are to be self controlled, not 'taken over' and therefore not responsible for their words. (Even the believer who prophesies in a ecstatic fashion as in a power-encounter prophecy is responsible for the words.) This is why we only 'release' those whom we know and with whom we are in relationship.

Personal prophetic words

The Scriptures place primary concern on the testing of prophets rather than prophecies, though both are commanded. In our fellowship we have many individuals who have been 'released' as members of the ministry team, as well as several others as trainees who are in the process of teaching, training and equipping. They are usually easily identified by a red 'ministry team' badge. You can be assured that those people, who from time to time minister with personal words to individuals, are under the authority and observation of the pastors who have responsibility for the spiritual oversight of the church. You may be confident, therefore, of their relative maturity and the trust which we have in them as loving stable Christians and able ministers.

There is still, however, the need to test all prophecies by the Spirit and the word since 'we prophesy in part'

(1 Corinthians 13:9), ie no prophecy or prophet is infallible or equal in authority to the Bible. Consider these guidelines when you receive a word.

Prophetic guidelines

1 Don't stifle or despise prophecy—test it (1 Thessalonians 5:19–22)

Though the prophecy may come in words or a style of delivery which you might not choose, or through a person to whom you may not relate well, consider their words as a word from God yet spoken by a man or a woman (1 Peter 4:11).

2 Does the prophecy conform to Scripture?

Words from the Spirit of God will always agree with his previous revelation in the Bible.

3 Does the Prophecy 'ring true' with your Spirit?

Usually a word will come to confirm what God has already spoken to you in various ways. It will confirm in you a certain direction and build your faith (John 10:2–5).

4 If there is an element of prediction, does it come true?

If there are factual statements which can be verified, are they accurate?

5 Does the prophecy bear good fruit in your life?

It is a principle of Scripture that a tree is judged by its fruit (Luke 6:43–45). If the prophecy is from the Holy Spirit, it will serve to glorify Jesus.

6 Wait on God for further confirmation and clarity.

Sometimes people try to use their prophetic gift to gain

recognition in the body of Christ. We as a church are much more interested in character than giftedness. Giftedness must flow out of wholeness, maturity and integrity. Sometimes 'would be' prophets will avoid all the church's safeguards and give you a word in the car park or some other private place. Avoid this like the plague!

Directional prophecy

Prophecies which give specific dates, times, life partners, relationships and exhortations to do or not to do something are reserved for the most mature and experienced, and even then, all of the above criteria apply. It is in these areas of dates and exact specifics that even the most 'gifted' may prove unreliable. Their word will be accurate, but often they will miss the time frame in which they expect something to happen.

About correction

Bringing correction is something that is reserved for the pastors, and definitely not for those who are new to prophecy or intercession. The Church is called to work together as a body, so those in leadership have the responsibility of keeping it all healthy. Beware of corrective, judgemental or condemning prophecy, as it will generally not be the Lord. Check it with the Lord, to hear from him and to live your life in the light of what he is personally saying to you.

Scriptures for you to consider

'Follow the way of love and eagerly desire spiritual gifts, especially the gift of prophecy' (1 Corinthians 14:1).

'Now about spiritual gifts, brothers, I do not want you to be ignorant' (1 Corinthians 12:1).

'To another miraculous powers, to another prophecy' (1 Corinthians 12:10).

'And in the church God has appointed first of all apostles, second prophets, third teachers, then workers of miracles, also those having gifts of healing, those able to help others, those with gifts of administration, and those speaking in different kinds of tongues' (1 Corinthians 12:28).

'Are all apostles? Are all prophets? Are all teachers? Do all work miracles?' (1 Corinthians 12:29).

'If I have the gift of prophecy and can fathom all mysteries and all knowledge, and if I have a faith that can move mountains, but have not love, I am nothing' (1 Corinthians 13:2).

'And now these three remain: faith, hope and love. But the greatest of these is love' (1 Corinthians 13:13).

'Follow the way of love and eagerly desire spiritual gifts, especially the gift of prophecy' (1 Corinthians 14:1).

'But everyone who prophesies speaks to men for their strengthening, encouragement and comfort' (1 Corinthians 14:3).

'He who speaks in a tongue edifies himself, but he who prophesies edifies the church' (1 Corinthians 14:4).

'I would like every one of you to speak in tongues, but I would rather have you prophesy. He who prophesies is greater than one who speaks in tongues, unless he interprets, so that the church may be edified' (1 Corinthians 14:5).

'Do not put out the Spirit's fire' (1 Thessalonians 5:19).

'Do not treat prophecies with contempt' (1 Thessalonians 5:20).

'Test everything. Hold on to the good' (1 Thessalonians 5:21).

NOTES

1 *USA TODAY* (Garnett Co., Inc.: Arlington, VA), 12 August 1992, editorial page.

2 Silvoso, Ed., *That None Should Perish* (Regal Books: Ventura, CA, 1994) pp. 57–96.

3 Yonggi Cho, David, *Patterns of Prayer* (Seoul Logos Co., Ltd.: Seoul, Korea, 1993), p. 26.

4 Gentile, Ernest B., 'Building Prophetic Churches', in Scheidler, Bill ed., *Perspectives* magazine (9200 NE, Freemont, Portland, Oregon).

5 Excerpt from Winkie Pratney's message at the conference 'Christian Equippers International', Washington, DC, 1987.

6 Sandford, John, *The Elijah Task* (Victory House: Tulsa, Oklahoma, 1997), p. 42.

7 Cooke, Graham, *Developing Your Prophetic Gifting* (Sovereign World Ltd.: Tonbridge, Kent, 1994), p. 191.

8 Guy Chevreau, *Praying with Fire* (HarperCollins: Toronto, Canada, 1995), pp. 32–101.

9 Sandford, John, *op. cit.*, pp. 154–155.

10 Excerpt from Dr Jack Deere's teaching during the 'Word of God with Power' conference, Toronto Airport Christian Fellowship, March 1994.

11 Kaufmann, Yehezel, trans. Greenberg, Moshe, *The Religion of Israel* (University of Chicago Press: Chicago, IL, 1960), p. 100.

12 Relf, Mary Stewart, *Cure of All Ills* (League of Prayer Press, 1988), p. 56.

13 Campbell, Wesley, *Welcoming a Visitation of the Spirit* (Creation House: Mary Lake, FLA, 1996), p. 90.

14 Ryle, James, *A Dream Come True* (Creation House: Mary Lake, FLA, 1995), pp. 66–69.

15 *Ibid.*, pp. 166–169.

16 Hayford, Jack, 'Signs of Imminate Grace', in Strang, Steven, ed., *Ministries Today* magazine (Creation House: Mary Lake, FLA), spring 1995.

17 Dr Winter's teaching at Pasadena World Missions Centre, Pasadena, California, emphasises that the conversion rate is now greater than the birth rate, among other facts on world revival.

18 Dawson, John, *Healing America's Wounds* (Regal Books: Ventura, CA, 1994), p. 297.

19 Douglas, J.D., ed., *The New Bible Dictionary* (Eerdmans Publishing: Grand Rapids, MI, 1971), pp. 537, 855.

20 Delitzsch, and Keil, C.F., *Commentary on the Old Testament* (Eerdmans Publishing: Grand Rapids, MI, 1976), vol. 1, p. 49.

21 Edwards, Gene, *State of the Arts* (Crossway Books: Wheaton, IL, 1991), pp. 19–20.

22 Schaeffer, Francis, *How Shall We Then Live?* (Crossway Books: Wheaton, IL, 1975), pp. 184–185.

23 Edwards, Gene, *op cit.*, p. 108.

24 Blomberg, David, *The Song of the Lord* (Bible Press: Portland, Oregon, 1978), p. 10.

25 Boschman, La Mar, *The Prophetic Song* (Destiny Image Publishers: Shippensberg, PA, 1986), p. 103.

26 *Ibid.*, p. 13.

27 Blomgren, David, *Prophetic Gatherings in the Church* (Bible Temple Publishing: Portland, Oregon, 1979), p. 27.

28 *Ibid.*, p. 27.

29 *Ibid.*, p. 28.

30 *Ibid.*, p. 29.

31 *Ibid.*, p. 29.

32 *Ibid.*, p. 29.

33 *Ibid.*, p. 29.

34 *Ibid.*, p. 29.

35 Grudem, Wayne, *The Gift of Prophecy* (Kingsway Publications, Eastbourne, 1990), p. 176.

36 Ervin Howard, *These Are Not Drunken* (Logos: Plainfield, NJ, 1969), p. 144.

37 Fee, Gordon, *God's Empowering Presence* (Hendrickson Publishers, Peabody, MASS, 1994), p. 892.

38 *Ibid.*, p. 891.

39 *Ibid.*, p. 891.

40 Riss, Richard, 'Tongues and Other Miraculous Gifts—Part 1', in *Basileia—Journal of Theology* (Mount Prospect, IL, 1990).

41 *Ibid.*, Part 4, p. 9.

42 *Ibid.*, Part 4, p. 11.

43 *Ibid.*, p. 128.

44 *Ibid.*, Part 1, p. 10.

45 *Ibid.*, Part 4, p. 11.

46 *Ibid.*, Part 2, p. 10.

47 Lange, John Peter, *The Gospel of John* (Charles Scribner and Sons: New York, 1884), p. 48.

48 *Basileia*, Part 4, p. 1.

49 *Ibid.*, Part 4, p. 11.

50 Bost, A., *Les Prophets Protestants* (Melun-Imprimere de Desrues, Paris, 1847), p. 82.

51 *Ibid.*, p. 148.

52 *Basileia*, Part 4, p. 1.

53 Bost, A., *op. cit.*, p. 51.

54 *Ibid.*, p. 188.

55 *Ibid.*, p. XIII.

56 Gali, Mark, *Christian History, Issue 45, Vol. XIV*, 'Cane Ridge', pp. 10–13 (Christianity Today, Carol Stream, IL).

57 *Ibid.*, p. 14.

58 Christian Literature Crusade (Ministry Report), *This Is That* (Richard Clay & Company, 1954), pp. 16–17.

59 Riss, Richard, *Latter Rain* (Honeycomb Visual Productions: Mississauga, ONT, 1980), p. 105.

60 *Ibid.*, p. 144.

BIBLIOGRAPHY

Chevreau, Guy, *Pray With Fire* (HarperCollins: London, 1995).

Cooke, Graham, *Developing Your Prophetic Gift* (Sovereign World, 1994).

Bickle, Mike, *Growing in the Prophetic* (Kingsway Publications: Eastbourne).

Fee, Gordon, *God's Empowering Presence* (Henrickson, 1988).

Grudem, Wayne, *The Gift of Prophecy* (Kingsway Publications: Eastbourne, 1988).

Sandford, John, *The Elijah Task* (Victory House, 1977).